INVENTORY 1985

INVENTORY 1985

# THE GADSDEN TREATY

# THE
# GADSDEN TREATY

PAUL NEFF GARBER, Ph.D

Sometime Harrison Fellow in History at the University of Pennsylvania
Instructor in History in Brown University

## A THESIS

Presented to the Faculty of the Graduate School in Partial
Fulfillment of the Requirements for the Degree of
Doctor of Philosophy in History

GLOUCESTER, MASS.

PETER SMITH

1959

To
My Father and My Mother
Samuel Garber
and
Ida A. Garber

# PREFACE

From the year 1821 to the present time, the American government has had to contend with what is commonly known as the "Mexican Question." It has entered into our national life to such an extent that it can almost be considered as one of our domestic problems. The platforms of the national parties bear witness to this fact, and each administration, often much to its discomfiture, has been forced to adopt some Mexican policy.

One of the many attempts of the American government to solve the Mexican question, was made in 1853, when President Pierce endeavoured to secure an amicable settlement of the issues then existing between the two nations. The Gadsden treaty was the result of his attempt. It is therefore the purpose of the author in this work to outline the factors that constituted the Mexican question in 1853; to study the influences that affected the negotiation and ratification of the treaty; and to explain the failure of the treaty to solve these problems. Considerable space has been devoted to the life and activities of the negotiator of the treaty, but I think no apology is necessary as the "Mexican Question" and the "Gadsden Question" were closely related during the administration of President Pierce.

I desire to express my deep obligation to Professor St. George L. Sioussat of the University of Pennsylvania for his aid, advice and helpful criticism in the preparation of this work. It was at his suggestion and under his guidance that this research was undertaken. Acknowledgment is also made of the valuable suggestions of Professors H. V. Ames, W. E. Lingelbach, and A. E. McKinley of the University of Pennsylvania. I am under especial obligation to Dr. Gaillard Hunt, Director of the Division of Publications of the Department of State, for granting me access to the archives of the Department of State; to Messrs. Devens and Stanton, of the Library of the Department of State, for their invaluable assistance; and to Mr. John C. Fitzpatrick, of the Division of Manuscripts of the Library of Congress for the many courtesies extended to me in my research. Acknowledgments are also due to Professor J. Fred Rippy of the University of Chicago for the use I have made of his research in this field; to Professor H. T. Collings of the University of Pennsylvania for his endeavours to secure materials in Mexico; to Mr. Lawrence C. Wroth, Librarian of The John Carter Brown Library, who has helped me in reading proof, and to whom I am indebted for many valuable suggestions. I am indebted to those members of the Gadsden family, who have in any way rendered assistance in the preparation of this work, but especially am I indebted to Mr. Paul Trapier Gadsden of Charleston, South Carolina.

PAUL NEFF GARBER

*Bridgewater, Virginia*
  *July 27, 1923*

# CONTENTS

# THE GADSDEN TREATY

# THE GADSDEN TREATY

## CHAPTER I

### INTRODUCTION

The history of American relations with the Mexican republic from its formation to the present time has been a record of constant diplomatic strife, and of an occasional resort to arms. The proximity of the two nations, in contrast with their differences in language, religion, psychology and political institutions, has at times rendered amicable relations impossible. The contact of the American nation with its sister republic has been a relationship between a progressive and a backward country. Out of this contact, problems of unusual significance have arisen, and the diplomatic settlement or solution thereof has been especially difficult.

One of the neglected topics in the diplomatic history of the two nations has been the Gadsden treaty. This subject has been almost unnoticed by most writers of general works and textbooks on American and Mexican history.[1] Unfortunately the history of American diplomatic relations with Mexico prior to 1861 has been colored by the same interpretation that was assigned many other events which occurred in the several decades before the Civil War, and only recently has historical scholarship exposed the falsity of the slavocracy theory in its application to Ameri-

---

[1] For example, McMaster, Rhodes, and Schouler each devote one paragraph to the subject.

can-Mexican relations.[2]  Wherever it has been discussed, the Gadsden treaty has been cited as another example of the attempts of the slaveholding states to acquire more territory for slavery.  But the use of new materials relating to the subject, through the opening of national archives, has made possible an approach from a new angle.

The background of the Gadsden treaty is found in the political and economic history of the United States and Mexico in the period from 1848 to 1853.  The point of departure is found in the treaty of Guadalupe Hidalgo, concluded February 2, 1848, between the two nations, which brought to an end the Mexican War.[3]  This war was the culmination of a series of misunderstandings on the part of both nations which dated from the formation of the Mexican republic.  After all attempts on the part of the United States to settle these difficulties had been defeated by the Mexican government, President Polk thought it necessary for the American government in May, 1846, to resort to arms to uphold the national dignity and interests, and to compel Mexico to fulfill her treaty obligations.  The Mexican War was therefore an attempt on the part of the President to settle by force all the then existing differences between the two nations.  The war, from the American standpoint, was from the beginning to the end inefficiently conducted, as the executive was harassed by a hostile Congress and had to contend with an insufficient army and jealous military commanders.  In general it may be said that the longer the war lasted, the more unpopular it became in the United States.

[2] Much credit is due Justin H. Smith for his valuable contribution to the knowledge of American-Mexican relations prior to 1849. In his two works, *The Annexation of Texas,* and *The War with Mexico,* he has given a new viewpoint on those much disputed questions.

[3] Malloy, W. M., *Treaties and Conventions,* I, 1107-1119.

The treaty of Guadalupe Hidalgo was framed and ratified in a manner similar to the conduct of the war. The
treaty, negotiated by representatives of a doubtful Mexican government and by a discredited American commissioner, contained germs of future discord between the two
countries. N. P. Trist, the American commissioner, appointed by President Polk to negotiate a treaty, acquired
only the minimum demands of his government upon
Mexico. The boundary line designated by the treaty and
accepted by President Polk was a compromise between
the demands of those who desired the absorption of all of
Mexico, and those who were opposed, on account of party
exigencies, hostility to slavery, or on general grounds, to
the annexation of any Mexican territory. Opposition to
the treaty on the part of each of these extreme factions
was so strong that in the Senate ratification was advised
by only a small margin of votes.[4] The treaty was also
opposed by prominent political parties in Mexico.[5] The
Puros, or radical party, desired the entire absorption of
Mexico by the United States. The Santanistas desired the
restoration of Santa Anna and were therefore hostile to
the party which had exiled their leader and made peace
with the United States. The Monarchists opposed any
action that might increase the power of the Republic.

By the treaty of Guadalupe Hidalgo Mexico recognized
the American view of the Rio Grande River as the boundary of Texas, and ceded to the United States Upper California and New Mexico, with the Gila River and an arbitrary line along the parallel of 32° north latitude as the

---

[4] The treaty was ratified by a vote of 38 to 14. A change of
four votes would have defeated the ratification. *S. Ex. Docs.* (509),
30 Cong., 1 sess., VII, no. 52, p. 36.

[5] In regard to the political parties in Mexico, see McCormac, E.
I., *James K. Polk*, 542–543; Rives, G. L., *The United States and
Mexico, 1821–1848*, II, 590–591, Smith, *The War with Mexico*, II,
2–4.

southern boundary of this cession. For this territory the
United States agreed to pay Mexico the sum of $15,000,000
and to release her from all American claims, acknowledged,
but never paid by that nation, prior to the negotiation
of the treaty. These claims, in addition to others, not
recognized by the Mexican government, were assumed by
the American government to the extent of three and a
quarter million dollars. The treaty provided for the suspension of hostilities; the withdrawal from Mexico of
American troops; the mutual exchange of prisoners of
war; the restoration of the Mexican custom-houses; and the
demarcation of the boundary line. Free navigation of
the Colorado and other rivers, and the use of Mexican soil
along the Gila River for the construction of a railroad or
canal were granted to the United States, and American
citizenship was promised to the inhabitants of the ceded
territory. By article XI the United States agreed to
protect Mexico from and to indemnify her for any injuries
inflicted on Mexican citizens by the Indians in the ceded
territory. The treaty of commerce of 1831 was renewed,
and both governments promised to settle in the future
their differences by pacific negotiations and arbitration.

President Polk remained in office only a short time after
the ratification of the treaty, yet before the close of his
term of office, he had taken some steps towards the carry-
ing out of its stipulations. Hostilities between the two
nations were stopped and on June 12, 1848, the American
flag was lowered in Mexico City.[6] Evacuation of Mexico
by the American troops, the exchange of prisoners of war,
and the restoration of custom-houses to the Mexican officials
took place in the summer of 1848. Diplomatic relations
were renewed by the appointment of Attorney-General

[6] Smith, *The War with Mexico*, II, 252.

Nathan Clifford as minister to Mexico.[7] A commissioner and surveyor were also appointed by President Polk to coöperate with Mexican officials in the location of the boundary line. The first installment of the $15,000,000 due Mexico, was paid by the Polk administration. On the last day of Polk's term of office, March 3, 1849, an act was passed by Congress, which provided for a commission to examine the claims of American citizens against Mexico, which under the treaty were assumed by the United States.[8]

During the years 1849-1853, the administrations under the guidance of Presidents Taylor and Fillmore, respectively, attempted to fulfill the remaining provisions of the treaty. The commission appointed to examine the American claims against Mexico concluded its work April 15, 1851.[9] On May 30, 1852, the last installment of the Mexican indemnity was paid. The territory which Mexico ceded by the treaty to the United States was organized in 1850 into the state of California and the territories of New Mexico and Utah.[10] The survey of the boundary line was continued. Attempts were made to control the Indians on the Mexican border, and thus prevent Indian inroads into Mexico, as was promised in article XI of the treaty.

Article XI and other matters connected with the treaty will receive further attention, but it is necessary first to indicate the political conditions which existed in the two nations, immediately after the Mexican War. In the United States the Democratic party was defeated in November 1848, and to the Whig party was entrusted the

[7] S. Ex. Journal, VIII, 462.

[8] U. S. Statutes at Large, IX, 353–354.

[9] Moore, J. B., History and Digest of International Arbitrations, II, 1253.

[10] U. S. Statutes at Large, IX, 446–458.

administration of foreign affairs. The acquisition of the vast domain from Mexico involved the country in perplexing and exciting questions in connection with slavery, and the administration was mainly absorbed with domestic affairs. Numerous changes also occurred in the Department of State and in the diplomatic service during the Whig administrations. Foreign affairs were directed successively by John M. Clayton, Daniel Webster and Edward Everett. This frequent change of officials in the Department of State and the fact that diplomatic affairs were subordinated to politics, account for the mediocre diplomacy of that period. Of the three Secretaries of State, Webster alone showed any aggressive attitude toward Mexican affairs.

The ministers to Mexico were untrained diplomats, and the diplomatic service suffered on that account. Ex-Governor R. P. Letcher of Kentucky, replaced Clifford as minister in August, 1849.[11] His mission was marked by a series of quarrels with the Mexican Minister of Foreign Relations, and with Secretary of State Webster. He detested Mexico, and his moral and political lectures were not appreciated by the Mexican government. His long furloughs to the United States placed the work of the embassy in the hands of the secretaries of the legation, Buckingham Smith and William Rich. Letcher was succeeded in August, 1852, by Alfred Conkling, Federal Judge of the Northern District of New York.[12] The diplomacy of Conkling added very little to the prestige of the United States in Mexico.

In Mexico, in contrast with the political situation in the United States, the leaders of the Mexican War, with the exception of Santa Anna, continued to control the government. The latter, after his military defeats in the war,

[11] *S. Ex. Journal*, VIII, 110.
[12] *Ibid.*, 423.

resigned as chief executive in September, 1847, but retained command of the army.[13] As the other leaders feared to leave him in control of the army, he was ordered to submit to a military trial. He chose rather to leave the country, and early in 1848 he departed from Mexico as an exile. After the resignation of Santa Anna, as chief executive, a provisional government was formed by Peña y Peña, which lasted until November 11, 1847, when General Anaya was elected President of the republic.[14] The term of the latter expired on January 8, 1848, and on that date, as no election had been held, the President of the Supreme Court, Peña y Peña, again assumed the executive power.[15] Under the administrations of Peña y Peña and Anaya, the treaty of Guadalupe Hidalgo was negotiated and ratified by the Mexican government.

The withdrawal of American troops from Mexico in the summer of 1848 left the Mexican people to work out alone their political destiny. In June, 1848, José Joaquin de Herrera was constitutionally elected President of the republic.[16] Herrera was one of the most capable political leaders of Mexico and had been the Mexican executive in 1846, when war with the United States began. Hostile political parties hindered his plans of reconstruction. Scarcely had he taken office, when his old enemy, General Paredes, started a revolution. Civil war also broke out in Yucatan. Financial reconstruction of the nation proved to be Herrera's greatest problem. The national debt was tremendous, and, except for the American indemnity, the Mexican Ministers of Finance had small means to carry out any financial program. It became difficult, therefore, to induce any prominent man to accept this

---

[13] Smith, *The War with Mexico,* II, 181–182.

[14] *Ibid.,* 180.

[15] Bancroft, H. H., *History of Mexico,* V, 535.

[16] *Ibid.,* 550.

office. From June, 1848 to January, 1851, there were sixteen different Ministers of Finance.[17] During Herrera's term of office, however, a semblance of government was maintained and all revolutionary attempts were suppressed.

Herrera was succeeded in January, 1851, by Arista, the repudiated general of the Mexican War.[18] As Minister of War under Herrera, he had gained a reputation for promoting strong national measures. Unfortunately, he entered office under unfavorable circumstances, when it was impossible to suppress further the revolutionary sentiment. Opposition to the government was increased by Arista's attempt to rehabilitate the treasury through curtailment of expenses and the enforcement of custom duties. By his friendly attitude toward the United States, and attempts at reconciliation, Arista further lost influence in Mexico.[19] *Pronunciamientos* increased, and by October, 1852, three-fourths of the states were in revolt against the national government.[20] Accordingly, on January 6, 1853, Arista resigned as President and Mexico was again controlled by a revolutionary party.[21]

During this period Mexico sent, as ministers to the United States, her best trained diplomats. Don Luis de la Rosa, one of Mexico's most distinguished statesmen, was the first minister sent after the war.[22] He had been Secretary of Foreign Relations in the Peña y Peña cabinet, and the establishment of peace between the two nations can be largely ascribed to his efforts. He was succeeded

[17] *Ibid.*, 566.

[18] *Ibid.*, 596–614.

[19] Smith to Webster, June 4, 1851, Dept. of State, Des., Mex., vol. 14, no. 61.

[20] Rich to Webster, Oct. 16, 1852, *ibid.*, vol. 15, no. 24.

[21] Conkling to Everett, Jan. 7, 1853, *ibid.*, vol. 16, no. 12.

[22] Rosa was received by President Polk, Dec. 2, 1848. Philadelphia *Public Ledger*, Dec. 5, 1848.

in May, 1852, by Manuel Larrainzar, who remained only a short time at Washington. Juan Almonte, who had been the Mexican minister to the United States at the outbreak of hostilities, replaced Larrainzar in 1853. His appointment was hailed as a harbinger of peace and understanding between the two countries.[23]

On the contrary, however, there continued in Mexico the former distrust and hatred of the United States. The raids of the filibusters and the attitude of American business men in Mexico increased the Mexicans' belief that the United States entertained sinister motives against their nation. The payment of the American indemnity to Mexico under the treaty of Guadalupe Hidalgo had a very demoralizing effect upon the finances of that country. A period of reckless finance followed and a feeling became prevalent in the official circles that money could always be obtained from the United States by the sale of Mexican territory.

If the feeling in Mexico was not friendly toward the United States, events had occurred in the latter nation, that presaged future disagreements and hostilities between the two countries. The decade following the Mexican War witnessed the rise of "Young America," and it was a period in which expansionist schemes were numerous. American capital was making itself felt abroad through foreign investments and by the opening of new avenues of commerce, especially in relation to trade with the Orient. The interest of American business men in Mexico was shown by their fight to control the payment of the American indemnity to that country. The discovery of gold in California, and the accompanying rush of population westward increased the demand for a safe and quick connection with the Pacific Coast. These, seemingly, were

[23] *Ibid.*, July 11, 1853.

American domestic problems, but they involved Mexican diplomacy because on Mexican soil, in contrast with the United States, were to be found short canal and more suitable railroad routes to the Pacific Ocean.

As has been indicated, by 1853 there was an outward semblance of reconciliation between the two nations, but on the other hand, there were diplomatic issues which had arisen out of the interpretation of the treaty of Guadalupe Hidalgo. Of the treaty in general, mention has already been made, but the particular articles which caused friction and induced diplomatic controversies were numbers five, six and eleven. They dealt with the survey of the boundary line between the two countries; the proposed railroad route; and the control by the American government of the Indians which inhabited the ceded Mexican territory. The question of an interoceanic communication by the way of the Isthmus of Tehuantepec, which had been omitted in the treaty, had also from 1848 on become an important issue. These questions proved to be the antecedents of the Gadsden treaty. Hence a minute discussion of each topic is necessary for an understanding of its negotiation and ratification.

# CHAPTER II

Article V of the treaty of Guadalupe Hidalgo provided for the location of the boundary line between the two countries.[1] According to this article the southeastern boundary line was to begin in the Gulf of Mexico, three leagues opposite the mouth of the Rio Grande, up the middle of that river, "to a point where it strikes the southern boundary of New Mexico (which runs north of the town called Paso) to its western termination, thence northward along the western line of New Mexico until it intersects the first branch of the river Gila." The southern and western limits of New Mexico were designated as those outlined in J. Disturnell's "Map of the United Mexican States." Both governments were to appoint a commissioner and surveyor to mark the boundary line. The result agreed upon by these commissioners and surveyors was to be considered a part of the treaty and was to have the same force as if it were inserted therein. The boundary was to be religiously respected by the two nations.

In accordance with the treaty, commissioners and surveyors were appointed by both governments. On December 18, 1848, President Polk nominated ex-Senator A. H. Sevier, of Arkansas, and Lieutenant A. B. Gray, of Texas, as commissioner and surveyor, respectively.[2] The nomination of Gray was confirmed by the Senate[3] but Sevier

---

[1] Malloy, *Treaties and Conventions*, I, 1109-1110.
[2] *S. Ex. Journal*, VIII, 8.

died, January 16, 1849, before the Senate had acted upon his nomination.  On January 16, 1849, Colonel John B. Weller, of Ohio, was nominated as commissioner by President Polk and the nomination was confirmed by the Senate.[4]  The Mexican representatives were Pedro Garcia Condé and José Salazar y Larregui.[5]

It was not until July, 1849, seventeen months after the signing of the treaty, that the members of the joint commission met at San Diego and this delay was only a sample of future difficulties.  The discovery of gold in California attracted all surplus labor, and the commissions found it difficult to retain their helpers.  After the Pacific demarcation was settled, the commissions disbanded to meet at El Paso in November, 1850.[6]  In the meantime Colonel Weller was removed, for political reasons, and was succeeded by Colonel John C. Frémont as commissioner.[7]  As the latter was elected United States Senator from California, he never joined the commission.[8]  John R. Bartlett, of Rhode Island, was then appointed commissioner, and under his leadership the boundary survey was commenced.[9]

It was in connection with the location of the initial point of the southeastern boundary line that a dispute arose between the American and Mexican commissions.  Bartlett arrived at El Paso, November 13, 1850, and on December 3, 1850, the first meeting with Garcia Condé was held.[10]  On account of errors in Disturnell's map, a prolonged discussion arose between the two commissioners in regard to the

3 *Ibid.*, 22.

4 *Ibid.*, 24.

5 *S. Ex. Docs.* (626), 32 Cong., 1 sess., XIV, no. 119, p. 56.

6 *Ibid.*, 65.

7 *S. Ex. Docs.* (558), 31 Cong., 1 sess., X, no. 34, p. 10.

8 *S. Ex. Docs.* (832), 34 Cong., 1 sess., XX, pt. 1, no. 108, p. 5.

9 *S. Ex. Journal*, VIII, 175.

10 *S. Ex. Docs.* (665), 32 Cong., 2 sess., VII, no. 41, p. 3.

southern boundary of New Mexico. It was ascertained by an astronomical examination that the town of El Paso was not situated on the parallel of 32° 15' north latitude, as marked by Disturnell, but on the parallel of 31° 45'. Thus, there was an error of half a degree in the map.[11] The question was, therefore, whether the southern boundary line should be located according to degrees of latitude and longitude or should be placed at a distance of eight miles above El Paso, as marked on the map. The second error was in relation to the course of the Rio Grande River, which was located on the map two degrees too far west.

Condé refused to accept the point eight miles above El Paso as marked by the map as the initial point for the survey. He demanded that the old boundary of New Mexico, 32° 20' north latitude, should be the southern line.[12] After four months of discussion, the matter was compromised in April, 1851. It was agreed that the Rio Grande struck the southern boundary of New Mexico at the parallel of 32° 21' north latitude, and instead of extending westward and terminating at the southwestern angle of New Mexico, which would give a line of but one degree to the United States, the southern line was prolonged three degrees toward the west, wherever it might run.[13]

By the terms of article V the commissioner and surveyor were invested with equal authority and were to agree on all decisions. Lieutenant Gray, the surveyor, was delayed by illness, and did not reach El Paso until July, 1851, three months after the Bartlett-Condé compromise had been con-

[11] Reports on the boundary line dispute by Commissioner Bartlett, Surveyor Gray, and Colonel Graham are found in *S. Ex. Docs.* (626), 32 Cong., 1 sess., XIV, no. 119; (665), 32 Cong., 2 sess., VII, no. 41; (667), 32 Cong., 1 sess., XV, no. 121; (752), 33 Cong., 2 sess., VII, no. 55.

[12] *S. Ex. Docs.* (626), 32 Cong., 1 sess., XIV, no. 119, p. 278.

[13] *S. Ex. Docs.* (665), 32 Cong., 2 sess., VII, no. 41, p. 3.

summated. In the meantime, Bartlett had appointed Lieutenant Whipple surveyor *ad interim,* and Whipple had agreed to the compromise.[14]  Gray, however, when asked by Bartlett to agree to the compromise, immediately refused, and protested against Bartlett's action.  He argued that the line should run on the surface of the earth, with reference to "the town called Paso," and with no regard to parallels of latitude.[15]  In this view Gray was correct, for in the negotiation of the treaty no specified parallel of latitude could be agreed upon by the commissioners and in order that Mexico might retain El Paso, it was finally decided to disregard all parallels and to take an arbitrary line just above the town, as marked on Disturnell's map.[16]

As Gray refused to assent to the new line, Bartlett suspended work on the southeastern boundary line and requested the Mexican commissioner to do likewise.[17]  Condé refused, and informed Bartlett that he would permit no measurements to be made in the territory of Mexico below the line of 32° 21′ north latitude.[18]  Thus the work of the boundary commission was at a standstill.

When this matter came to the attention of the authorities at Washington, the administration took the side of Bartlett.  Gray was ordered to sign the Bartlett-Condé agreement, and, on his refusal, was recalled.[19]  He was succeeded by Colonel W. H. Emory, who was likewise ordered to sign the agreement.  Emory did so, but attached a proviso,

[14] *Ibid.,* 14.

[15] *S. Ex. Docs.* (752), 33 Cong., 2 sess., VII, no. 55, p. 6.

[16] *S. Ex. Docs.* (626), 32 Cong., 1 sess., XIV, no. 119, pp. 298–299.

[17] *Ibid.*

[18] Condé to Bartlett, Aug. 3, 1851, Dept. of State, Des., Mex., vol. 15, with no. 100.

[19] *S. Ex. Docs.* (626), 32 Cong., 1 sess., XIV, no. 119, p. 121.

which declared the line to be merely the boundary agreed upon by the two commissioners and nothing else. He did this, as he later stated, "to leave the government free to act, and repudiate the agreement by the two commissioners." [20]

The Bartlett-Condé line was upheld by the Whig administration. Secretary of the Interior Stuart, in his report to President Fillmore, July 24, 1851, said that if the compromise had not been made, it would have resulted either in a failure to run any line or in the loss of valuable gold and silver mines and a sacrifice of more territory than would be lost under the other line.[21] To recede now from the line agreed upon by the commissioners, he declared, was incompatible with the terms of article V, which said that the results agreed upon by the commissioners should be a part of the treaty and could not be altered without the consent of both nations. President Fillmore agreed with Secretary Stuart in this interpretation of the treaty.

This view was not acceptable to the Democratic leaders of the Senate, especially those from California and Texas. Weller, of California, the former boundary commissioner demanded an investigation of Bartlett's conduct.[22] Rusk, of Texas, declared, July 6, 1852, that he would never vote another dollar for the survey until he was assured that the treaty of Guadalupe Hidalgo and not the negotiations between the commissioners would settle the initial point.[23] Mason, of Virginia, asserted that, whether right or wrong, the boundary of the United States was to be governed by

---

[20] *S. Ex. Docs.* (832), 34 Cong., 1 sess., XX, pt. 1, no. 108, p. 17.

[21] *S. Ex. Docs.* (688), 33 Cong., Special sess., I, no. 6, p. 10.

[22] *Cong. Globe*, 32 Cong., 1 sess. (1851–52), XXIV, pt. 2, p. 1628.

[23] *Ibid.*, 1660.

the lines marked on the treaty map and not by lines of latitude.[24]

The Senate, by a resolution, called on President Fillmore to furnish all the instructions and correspondence on the subject.[25]  On August 30, 1852, Senator Mason, chairman of the Committee on Foreign Relations, reported a series of resolutions which disagreed with the view held by the administration.[26]  These resolutions asserted that the commissioners and surveyors had no authority to vary or modify the boundary line and that authority on all matters was conferred jointly on the commissioner and surveyor. The act of Bartlett, by the establishment of a new boundary line, in disregard of the one designated on the map, was declared to be a departure from the treaty.  On August 31, 1852, Congress appropriated $100,000 for the boundary survey, but with a proviso that no part of the sum should be used until the southern boundary was established according to the line laid down in Disturnell's map.[27]  This halted further operations of the boundary commission.

The changed boundary line involved the Mesilla valley, as shown by the accompanying map.  The boundary line as designated in the treaty would have been located thirty miles south of the Bartlett-Condé line.  Five or six thousand square miles of territory were thereby lost to the United States.[28]  This valley had been settled in 1848 by Americans and Mexicans, and by 1853 it contained a population of three thousand persons.[29]  A great part of the region was arid and unproductive, although some good land

[24] *S. Reports* (631), 32 Cong., 1 sess., II, no. 345, p. 3.

[25] *Cong. Globe,* 32 Cong., 1 sess. (1851–52), XXIV, pt. 1, p. 814.

[26] *S. Reports* (631), 32 Cong., 1 sess., II, no. 345.

[27] *U. S. Statutes at Large,* X, 94–95.

[28] Washington *Union,* May 7, 1853.

[29] Mansfield to Meriwether, Oct. 25, 1853, Dept. of State, Misc. Let.

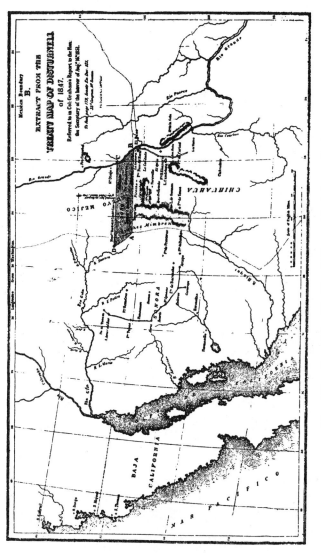

Map. No. I.    The Mesilla Valley.   (shaded portion)
Line A–B.    Original treaty line.
Line C–D.    Bartlett-Condé line.

was available along the Ascequia River. The agricultural value of this territory was insignificant. Consequently, the loss of the Mesilla valley might have been overlooked, and the Bartlett-Condé compromise accepted by the United States, had it not been for a vital issue then before the country, namely, the question of a transcontinental railroad.

The idea of a railroad to the Pacific Coast had been suggested by several individuals in the beginning of the period of railroad construction in the United States.[30] Prior to 1845, however, all such suggestions were vague speculations. The primary object of the agitation for a transcontinental railroad was to facilitate commercial relations with Asia. This was the motive that influenced Asa Whitney, the pioneer in this field.

Asa Whitney, a merchant of New York City, played an important part in arousing popular interest in the construction of a transcontinental railroad. In January, 1845, he memorialized Congress for a grant of public domain, to aid the construction of a railroad to the Pacific. His original scheme was to build the railroad on a route from the Great Lakes westward. His plan was before the public from 1845 to 1852. Whitney's project was favorably recommended by congressional committees no less than seven times and it was supported by petitions, resolutions of public meetings and state legislatures. By 1850 the systematic lobbying of Whitney and his associates had educated the public to an acceptance of the railway idea.

Whitney's plan for a northern route was followed by a rival project for a southern route to the Pacific. The period between 1840 and 1850 was characterized by rail-

---

[30] For a good discussion of the early plans for a transcontinental railroad, see Albright, G. L., *Official Explorations for Pacific Railroads, 1853–1855*, 1–43.

road-building in the southern states.[31]     An attempt was made by the seaboard cities to revive their dwindling commerce by means of railroad connections to the Mississippi River.  Agitation for a railroad to the Pacific Coast, to tap the trade of the Orient, naturally followed.  Among the first advocates of a strictly southern route were Robert Patterson and Professor Forshey, of Louisiana, and Colonel James Gadsden, President of the South Carolina Railroad Company.[32]

The plan for a southern route had been suggested even before the Mexican War.  In a report at the Memphis Convention of 1845, Gadsden had recommended a southern route, through the state of Texas and along the Gila River in Mexican territory.[33]  In the annual report of 1845 to the stockholders of the South Carolina Railroad Company, he again advocated a southern route.[34]  He recommended as the western terminus, the city of Mazatlan on the Gulf of California.

The war with Mexico and the certain acquisition of Mexican territory by the United States brought the subject of a transcontinental railroad into the peace negotiations.

---

[31] Cotterill, R. S., "Memphis Railroad Convention, 1849," in *Tenn. His. Mag.*, IV, 83.  For a further discussion of the movement for a southern transcontinental railroad, see Cotterill, R. S., "Early Agitation for a Pacific Railroad, 1845–50," in *Miss. Val. His. Rev.*, V, 366–415; "Southern Railroads and Western Trade, 1840–50," in *Miss. Val. His. Rev.*, III, 427–441; Mayes, E., "Origin of the Pacific Railroads, and especially of the Southern Pacific," in *Pub. of the Miss. His. Soc.*, VI, 307–337; Sioussat, St. G. L., "Memphis as a Gateway to the West," in *Tenn. His. Mag.*, III, 1–28; 77–115; "Southern Projects for a Railroad to the Pacific Coast, 1845–1857," an unpublished paper read before the American Historical Association at New Haven, Connecticut, December 29, 1922.

[32] Albright, *Official Explorations*, 11.

[33] *De Bow's Commercial Review*, Jan. 1846 (I, 27–33).

[34] *Ibid.*, May 1847 (III, 447); June 1847 (III, 485).

In June 1847 De Bow declared: "We are at war with Mexico, and probably shall dictate our own terms of peace. The right of way for a railroad through such regions of Mexico to the Pacific as we see desirable should be by all means exacted."[35]   Secretary of State Buchanan directed Trist to procure from Mexico the entire valley of the Gila River, because it presented a favorable route for a railroad to the Pacific.[36]   Trist was unable to get this concession, but by article VI of the treaty it was stipulated that if, in the future, a road, canal, or railroad should be constructed which should run along the Gila River, within the radius of one marine league of either the right or the left bank, the two countries were to form an agreement as to its construction.[37]

After the close of the war, interest in a transcontinental railroad became more intense.   This increase of interest was due to the settlement of the Oregon question, the acquisition of California and New Mexico from Mexico in 1848, and the discovery of gold in California in 1849. In order to defend California and to keep her in the Union, a quick connection between the East and the West was necessary.

A period of railway expansion followed the war.   Railroad mileage rose from 8,800 miles in 1850 to 21,300 miles in 1854.[38]   In 1850 Congress began on a large scale the policy of granting public lands to the states to encourage railroad construction.   This period of railroad expansion further aided the plan of a transcontinental railroad to the Pacific Coast.

[35] *Ibid.*, June 1847 (III, 478).

[36] Buchanan to Trist, July 13, 1847, *S. Ex. Docs.* (509), 30 Cong., 1 sess., VII, no. 52, p. 90.

[37] Malloy, *Treaties and Conventions*, I, 1111.

[38] McMaster, J. B., *A History of the People of the United States*, VIII, 88.

The acquisition of New Mexico and California made possible the construction of a southern transcontinental railroad upon American soil. Greater interest in such a road was accordingly aroused. While the southern states were at odds with one another over the eastern terminus, they all agreed that the western route was through Texas and along the Gila River, near the thirty-second parallel of north latitude. This was the route recommended by the Memphis Commercial Convention of 1849.[39] Military officials located on the southwestern frontier strongly recommended the southern route. Captain R. B. Marcy in 1848 reported that, "any experienced and impartial engineer, after a thorough and careful reconnaissance of all the different routes would at once give this the preference over any other." [40] Major P. St. George Cooke, who traversed the Gila region in 1848, said that it was the best route because of many reasons, in addition to the "weighty consideration that a railroad would prove the only effective barrier to the attacks on Mexico by the predatory Indians of the North." [41]

The importance of the southern route was also stressed because it would aid the fulfillment of treaty stipulations with Mexico. A special commission was appointed, in October, 1850, to obtain statistics and make treaties with the Indian tribes along the border of the United States and Mexico.[42] This commission, composed of C. J. Todd, Oliver Temple, and R. B. Campbell, recommended, in August, 1851, the construction of a railroad along the southern boundary of the United States as a means to control the

---

[39] *De Bow's Commercial Review*, March 1850 (VIII, 229); *H. Reports* (585), 31 Cong., 1 sess., III, no. 439, pp. 12–13.
[40] *S. Ex. Docs.* (562), 31 Cong., 1 sess., XIV, no. 54, pp. 225–226.
[41] Washington *Union*, Dec. 10, 1848.
[42] *S. Ex. Docs.* (587), 31 Cong., 2 sess., I, no. 1, p. 153.

Indians in that region.[43] A railroad contiguous to the boundary line was regarded as especially advantageous for the fulfillment of treaty stipulations with Mexico. Duff Green had a scheme to manipulate the payments of the Mexican indemnity so that a large grant of land, which included the valley of the Gila River, could be bought of Mexico. He informed Secretary Clayton that if his agent should secure such a grant, "the (rail) road will soon be made, and the grant densely inhabited; in which case the American population on that land will give to the Mexicans ample protection from the American Indians, and thus relieve the United States from a large expenditure now required by the Mexican Treaty." [44]

The American government also was interested in a southern route. The boundary commission was directed to examine and survey the Gila River region, with a view to ascertain the practicability of a road, canal, or railroad through that section. Buchanan informed Weller that "the inquiry is one of great importance to the country, and any information which you can communicate to the department on the subject will be highly appreciated by our fellow citizens." [45] Bartlett, when he organized his commission, required an additional force in order to make the survey of a route for a road or railway.[46] So much of the time of the American commission was spent in this survey that the Mexican minister at Washington was compelled to protest to Secretary Webster. Rosa declared that if such work

[43] *S. Ex. Docs.* (613), 32 Cong., 1 sess., III, no. 1, pp. 302–306.

[44] Green to Clayton, March 12, 1850, *Cong. Globe*, 32 Cong., sess. (1851–52), XXIV, pt. 1, p. 339.

[45] Buchanan to Weller, Jan. 24, 1849; Feb. 13, 1849, *S. Ex. Docs.* (558), 31 Cong., 1 sess., X, no. 34, pp. 2–3.

[46] Bartlett, J. R., *Personal Narrative of Explorations*, I, 5.

were continued, the location of the boundary line could not be concluded in less than five years.[47]

When Lieutenant Gray objected to the Bartlett-Condé line, he was influenced by motives other than the mere retention of the Mesilla valley by the United States. Gray was a native of Texas, and had served on the Texas-Louisiana boundary commission of 1840–1841.[48] He was interested in a southern railroad route to the Pacific through his state, and at times had served as engineer for eastern railroad companies which were promoting such a road. He considered that the surrender of the Mesilla valley to Mexico would result in the loss of the only practicable railroad route to the Pacific through American territory. In his official report on the survey, he declared that the Mesilla valley, from the standpoint of territory, was of little value, but that this disputed region embraced the most accommodating gateway over the Rocky Mountains and the most feasible railroad route from the Rio Grande to California.[49]

Bartlett denied that his boundary line deprived the United States of the most practicable route for a railroad to the Pacific. He was supported in this view by the other members of the commission, with the exception of Gray. Lieutenant Whipple declared that it would be impossible to construct a road to run wholly along the Gila River, as it was necessary to enter the state of Sonora in order to avoid the Pinal Llano Mountains.[50] Colonel Emory reported that the line advocated by Bartlett was as valuable for a railroad as that championed by Gray, but that any practicable route must go south of both of these bound-

[47] Rosa to Webster, March 11, 1851, *S. Ex. Docs.* (627), 32 Cong., 1 sess., XV, no. 120, p. 1.

[48] Marshall, T. M., *A History of the Western Boundary of the Louisiana Purchase, 1819–1841*, 237.

[49] *S. Ex. Docs.* (752), 33 Cong., 2 sess., VII, no. 55, p. 28.

[50] *S. Ex. Docs.* (665), 32 Cong., 2 sess., VII, no. 41, p. 20.

ary lines.[51]   A study of the physical geography of the region supports these views.

These reports were overlooked by the friends of the southern transcontinental railroad.   They accepted the view of Gray, that the Bartlett line forfeited the best route for a railway, while the other boundary would include it. The greatest protest against the loss of the Mesilla valley came from the state of Texas.   On June 28, 1852, the congressmen of Texas protested against the new boundary line.[52]   They declared that it would necessarily create a most serious impediment to the construction of a road to the Pacific at any future time.   In August, 1852, they protested to Secretary Stuart against the discarding of Disturnell's map, because the line run in accordance with that map would "throw into the territory of the United States the best route that is to be found for a road to connect the valley of the Mississippi with the shores of the Pacific Ocean." [53]   Senator Mason, of Virginia, reported that the loss of the most practicable route to the Pacific was of greater importance in the opinion of the Committee on Foreign Relations than any loss of territory.[54]

During the years 1851–1853, Congress devoted much time and attention to the subject of a transcontinental railroad. Many projects were proposed and debated and in the second session of the Thirty-Second Congress (1852–1853), the Senate gave more time to the discussion of that topic than to all other subjects.[55]   The rivalry between the North and South over the proposed route was so intense that Congress was unable to take any action.   The increase of sectionalism due to the growth of the slavery controversy

[51] *S. Ex. Docs.* (832), 34 Cong., 1 sess., XX, pt. 1, no. 108, p. 17.
[52] *S. Ex. Docs.* (688), 33 Cong., Special sess., I, no. 6, p. 142.
[53] *S. Ex. Docs.* (627), 32 Cong., 1 sess., XV, no. 121, p. 88.
[54] *S. Reports* (631), 32 Cong., 1 sess., II, no. 345, p. 4.
[55] Davis, J. P., *The Union Pacific Railway*, 44.

further hindered the construction of the railroad. The only result of months of animated debate in Congress upon the Pacific railway was a clause in the army appropriation bill of March 3, 1853.[56] By this article an appropriation of $150,000 was made for surveys to ascertain the most practicable and economical route for a railroad from the Mississippi River to the Pacific Ocean.

The advocates of the southern route now became more aggressive. After the adjournment of Congress, March 3, 1853, Senator Rusk, of Texas, made a tour of inspection for a southern route.[57] In a speech at San Antonio, Texas, he declared that the southern route was the best, as it was the most direct connection to the Pacific and was located in the most feasible territory.[58] The Southern Commercial Convention, which met at Memphis, June, 1853, resolved that, as the government could build only one road to the Pacific, it should be located on the route which combined in the greatest degree the advantages of genial climate, cheapness of construction, and accessibility at all seasons from all portions of the Union.[59] Governor Bell, in his message to the Texas legislature, November, 1853, recommended legislation for the construction of a railroad through Texas. He pointed out that the best track for a Pacific railroad should begin at Memphis or some nearby point, enter Texas about the thirty-second parallel of north latitude, pursue that line to El Paso or its neighborhood, thence in the direction of the headwaters of the Gila River, and down the river by the most practicable route to San Diego on the Pacific Ocean.[60] An act was passed by the Texas legislature, December 21, 1853, which provided for the construc-

---

[56] *U. S. Statutes at Large*, X, 219.
[57] Texas *State Gazette*, Sept. 24, 1853.
[58] New Orleans *Daily Picayune*, Dec. 4, 1853.
[59] *De Bow's Review*, Sept. 1853 (XV, 267).
[60] *Journal of the Texas House of Rep.*, 1853–54, p. 17.

tion of the Mississippi and Pacific Railroad on the route recommended by Governor Bell.[61]

Thus the Bartlett-Condé boundary line dispute involved more than simply a few thousand square miles of valueless land. The boundary line was undetermined because the Mexican commissioner would not accept new proposals, and the United States Congress refused to appropriate money for any survey except for the boundary line as marked on Disturnell's map. Five years had elapsed since the negotiation of the treaty, and in the meantime the disputed territory, the Mesilla valley, was claimed by both countries. Such a condition would inevitably lead to a clash of arms should either nation attempt to possess the region. The friends of the southern railroad route were determined to retain the disputed region, because it aided their project. At the same time the supporters of the central and northern transcontinental routes looked with disfavor upon the rival route, and were lukewarm in their support of the Mesilla contention. Consequently the new administration which came into power on March 4, 1853, had a boundary dispute to settle with Mexico which was complicated by a domestic sectional question.

Article XI of the treaty of Guadalupe Hidalgo was closely related to the boundary question and had likewise, soon after the ratification of the treaty, become a point of issue between the two countries. By this article, the United States agreed to provide for the Indians which were located in the territory ceded by Mexico, and also to protect Mexico from them.[62] The United States was to restrain all incursions by these Indians into Mexico, and, when unable to check these inroads, the American government was to punish the Indians and exact satisfaction ''with

---

[61] Texas *State Gazette,* Feb. 7, 1854.
[62] Malloy, *Treaties and Conventions,* I, 1112–1113.

equal diligence and energy as if same incursions were meditated or committed within its own territory against its own citizens.'' Citizens of the United States were forbidden to purchase any goods which were stolen in Mexico by these Indians, and in case persons were captured and brought into the United States, the government was to rescue them and return them to an agent of the Mexican government. The United States was "to pass without unnecessary delay and always vigilantly enforce such laws as the nature of the subject may require.''

In view of the later difficulty to enforce this article, it appears strange that such a provision was accepted by the American negotiator. But, as early as 1845, Secretary Buchanan had instructed Slidell to include such a clause in the proposed treaty with Mexico.[63] Buchanan thought that the province of New Mexico should be included within the limits of the United States, as this cession would relieve Mexico of the trouble and expense of defending its citizens against the Indians in that region. He informed Slidell that if New Mexico were ceded, it would at once become the duty of the American government to restrain the savage tribes within that region, and to prevent any hostile incursions into Mexico. Slidell was unable to make a treaty, but his successor, Trist, included such an article in his treaty with Mexico.

This article, Trist informed Buchanan, was necessary to make the treaty acceptable to the northern states of Mexico.[64] To Trist it meant nothing more than article XXIII of the Commercial treaty of 1831, but it was set forth in detail to satisfy the Mexican public. The exact fulfill-

[63] Buchanan to Slidell, Nov. 10, 1845, *S. Ex. Docs.* (509), 30 Cong., 1 sess., VII, no. 52, p. 78.

[64] Trist to Buchanan, Jan. 25, 1848, *ibid.*, 293.

[65] Rippy, J. F., "A Ray of Light on the Gadsden Treaty," in *Southwestern His. Quar.*, XXIV, 238–239.

ment of the article, Trist declared, involved impossibilities. Santa Anna later stated that is was included in the treaty only that the horrible sacrifice of half of the territory of the republic for $15,000,000 might not appear too prominent a feature.[65] He regarded the article as a farce, because the United States had no interest in the protection of the frontier and Mexico could not compel such protection. Further, he declared that it was a humiliating clause for it begged the United States, the worst enemy of Mexico, to do a national service.

When the treaty was presented in the Senate for ratification, Senator Houston, of Texas, moved that it be rejected because it provided neither indemnity for the past nor security for the future.[66] The enforcement of article XI, he stated, would be worth more, from a pecuniary point of view, than all the vacant lands acquired from Mexico. Senator Douglas, of Illinois, moved that the part of the article which bound the United States to indemnify Mexican sufferers for Indian damages be struck out, but the motion was defeated by a vote of 5 to 47.[67] Thus article XI was accepted in good faith by the Senate. Secretary Buchanan declared that, ''the government possessed both the ability and will to restrain the Indians within the limits of the United States from making incursions into the Mexican territory as well as to execute all the other stipulations of the eleventh article.'' [68]

In the five years that followed 1848, the United States showed its inability to enforce this stipulation of the treaty. Such enforcement was especially difficult because of the large number of Indians who were located near the Mexican border. Within the territory acquired from

[66] *S. Ex. Docs.* (509), 30 Cong., 1 sess., VII, no. 52, p. 5.
[67] *Ibid.*
[68] *Ibid.*, 70.

Mexico were some 160,000 Indians.[69]   There were 45,000
in the territory of New Mexico, which bordered on Mexico,
and they were not peace-loving Indians.[70]   The Apaches
and Comanches were located usually along the boundary
line, with the Navajos to the north of them in the central
part of the territory of New Mexico and still farther north
were the Utahs.[71]   In addition to these, there were 29,000
Indians in Texas.[72]   The Indians along the Arkansas River,
the northern Comanches, Kioways, and others, were leagued
with their southwestern brethren.   They either took part in
the annual predatory raids into Mexico or helped to dispose of the plunder.[73]

The most warlike of these Indians were the Apaches.   Ever
since the Spanish conquest they had waged a predatory
war upon the settlers of New Spain.   Although the
Apaches were gradually pushed north by the Spanish into
desolate wilds, a guerilla warfare had existed between them
for centuries.[74]   This hostility and mutual hatred had been
bequeathed by the Spanish to the Mexican government.
Moreover, acts of treachery had been practiced by the Mexicans against the Apaches, and, though the years passed
by, these acts were not forgotten by the Indians.[75]   Naturally, when they became wards of the United States, they
did not suddenly change their warlike habits.

Between 1848 and 1853 Indian outrages were per-
petrated both in New Mexico and Mexico.   Indian Agent
Graves, of New Mexico, reported in August, 1853, that,

---

[69] *S. Ex. Docs.* (690), 33 Cong., 1 sess., I, no. 1, p. 60.

[70] *Ibid.*

[71] *H. Misc. Docs.* (741), 33 Cong., 1 sess., I, no. 38, p. 5.

[72] *S. Ex. Docs.* (690), 33 Cong., 1 sess., I, no. 1, p. 60.

[73] *Ibid.*, 253.

[74] *U. S. and Mexican Claims Commission, 1868*, Briefs, II, no. 131,
p. 9.

[75] *S. Ex Docs.* (626), 32 Cong., 1 sess., XIV, no. 119, p. 421.

"since annexation of this territory to the United States, they (Jicarilla Apaches) have committed acts of murder, robbery, and other crimes which in savage brutality stand without a parallel in history." [76] Governor Meriwether, of New Mexico, declared in 1853 that scarcely a day passed without the commission of some theft, robbery, or murder by the Indians. [77] Two companies of infantry were sent to protect the boundary survey commission from the Indians, but they proved inadequate for the task. The Indians attacked both the commission and the escort, and at one time they had stolen every available horse and mule from both camps. [78] In Mexico, where there was less resistance, the damages and cruelty of the Indians far surpassed that in New Mexico. Of their barbarity in Mexico, Bartlett stated that, "the extent of the depredations and murders committed by them would be appalling if summed up." [79]

After the ratification of the treaty, the United States immediately attempted to enforce the provisions of article XI. The greater part of the army was posted in the territory acquired from Mexico. The articles of the treaty were published in General Orders No. 49, of August 31, 1848, and again in No. 17, of March 26, 1849, and were distributed to every military commander for his information. [80] In his annual message to Congress, December, 1849, President Taylor recommended an increase of several corps of the army at the distant western posts to enforce the treaty obligations with Mexico. [81] General P. F. Smith, of the Texas Military Department, and Colonel E. V. Sumner, of the New Mexico Military Department, were

[76] S. Ex. Docs. (690), 33 Cong., 1 sess., I, no. 1, p. 434.
[77] Ibid., 430.
[78] S. Ex. Docs. (626), 32 Cong., 1 sess., XIV, no. 119, p. 173.
[79] Bartlett, Personal Narrative, I, 5.
[80] Davis to Marcy, Dec. 29, 1854, Dept. of State, Misc. Let.
[81] S. Ex. Docs. (549), 31 Cong., 1 sess., I, no. 1, p. 13.

ordered to protect the territory of Mexico as well as that of the United States from Indian depredations.[82]    In the selection of their posts they were to be governed by these orders.    In 1852, of the 11,000 soldiers in the army, nearly 8,000 were employed in the defense of the newly acquired territory and Texas.[83]    Five thousand soldiers were stationed exclusively along the southern border of Texas and New Mexico.[84]    The military expenditures of the territory of New Mexico from 1848 to 1853 amounted to a sum of $12,000,000.[85]    The expenses for the transportation of troops and supplies increased from $130,053.52 in 1845 to $2,994,408.51 in 1851.[86]    Jefferson Davis, Secretary of War, declared in 1854 that the government in its solicitude to enforce the article had overlooked the claims of its own citizens, by the withdrawal of troops from other points of danger to the Mexican border.[87]

The Department of the Interior, created in 1849, was given control of Indian affairs.    This department, through the Commissioner of Indian Affairs, also attempted to assist in the enforcement of article XI but its efforts were delayed and proved to be very ineffective.    On April 7, 1849, a copy of the treaty was sent to James S. Calhoun, Indian Agent for New Mexico.[88]    He was instructed to employ the best means in his power to enforce the stipulations.    On September 9, 1849, Calhoun made a treaty with the Navajoes and on December 30, 1849, a treaty was negotiated with the Utahs.[89]    These treaties provided for

[82] *S. Ex. Docs.* (611), 32 Cong., 1 sess., I, no. 1, pp. 117, 125.

[83] *S. Ex. Docs.* (549), 31 Cong., 1 sess., I, no. 1, p. 13.

[84] *S. Ex. Docs.* (691), 33 Cong., 1 sess., II, no. 1, p. 95.

[85] *S. Ex. Docs.* (690), 33 Cong., 1 sess., I, no. 1, p. 437.

[86] *U. S. and Mex. Claims Commission, 1868*, Briefs, II, no. 131, p. 24.

[87] Davis to Marcy, Dec. 29, 1854, Dept. of State, Misc. Let.

[88] Stuart to Webster, June 12, 1851, Webster Papers, vol. 10.

[89] *U. S. Statutes at Large*, IX, 974–984.

the designation by the United States at its earliest convenience of territorial limits for each of these tribes. But by 1853 no designation of limits had been made. Upon the recommendation of the Secretary of the Interior, Congress, on September 30, 1850 had appropriated $30,000 for the purpose of collecting information and making treaties with the Indians of the southwest.[90] Three agents, Todd, Temple, and Campbell, were appointed, who accompanied the boundary commission.[91] In 1851, the Department of the Interior urged Congress to appropriate an additional $50,000 to carry on this work. This, Congress refused to do, and accordingly the three agents were recalled without the negotiation of any treaties.[92] However, on July 1, 1852, Colonel E. V. Sumner, of the New Mexico Military Department, made a treaty with the Apaches, and Indian Agent Fitzpatrick made a treaty with the Comanches and Kiowas of the region of the Arkansas River.[93]

These treaties were of little value, as they were not observed by the Indians, nor did the government assign to the Indians territorial limits as was stipulated. The Indian agents were unable to control their wards on the frontier. Secretary Stuart, on November 29, 1851, admitted that the efforts of the Department of the Interior had been without success.[94] Indian Agent Graves declared in 1853 that the Indian policy of New Mexico as administered up to that time had been a failure, as it gave protection to neither life nor property.[95]

The enforcement of article XI by the government had proved to be an impossibility as Trist had prophesied.

[90] *Ibid.*, 556.
[91] *S. Ex. Docs.* (587), 31 Cong., 2 sess., I, no. 1, p. 153.
[92] Stuart to Webster, June 12, 1851, Webster Papers, vol. 10.
[93] *U. S. Statutes at Large*, X, 979–981; 1013–1015.
[94] *H. Ex. Docs.* (635), 32 Cong., 1 sess., II, pt. 2, no. 2, p. 502.
[95] *S. Ex. Docs.* (690), 33 Cong., 1 sess., I, no. 1, p. 436.

There were too many difficulties to overcome. In regard to the Indians themselves, there was no incentive to stop their predatory raids into Mexico. These Indian tribes had no special homes. They simply followed the chase or made predatory raids, as their movements were governed by the seasons. They were located along a boundary line of two thousand miles, part of which was not designated, and the country along the border offered as Secretary of War Conrad said, "wonderful facilities to escape and insurmountable barriers to pursue." [96] To escape the American troops, the Indians crossed the boundary line into Mexico where American troops had no authority to go. An attempt was made by the American government to obtain permission from Mexico to pursue the Indians into Mexican territory, but this proposal was rejected as a national insult.[97] Every effort on the part of the army to punish these Indians simply drove them into Mexico, as they went where the least resistance was offered.[98]

The Indian policy of Mexico made still more difficult the enforcement of this article. In order to prevent revolutions in the northern states of Mexico, the government disarmed the inhabitants after the treaty of Guadalupe Hidalgo and left them, until the fall of 1853, without the means to protect themselves from the Indians.[99] As a means of protection to the frontier, a decree was issued July 19, 1848, for the establishment of eighteen military colonies along the entire American border.[100] No attempt was made

[96] *S. Ex. Docs.* (611), 32 Cong., 1 sess., I, no. 1, p. 105.

[97] Marcy to Almonte, Feb. 4, 1856, Dept. of State, Notes from Dept., Mex. Leg., vol. 7.

[98] *S. Ex. Docs.* (611), 32 Cong., 1 sess., I, no. 1, p. 18.

[99] Gadsden to Bonilla, Sept. 9, 1853, Dept. of State, Des., Mex., vol. 18, with no. 4.

[100] Bancroft, H. H., *History of the North Mexican States and Texas*, II, 612.

to enforce this decree, however, until July, 1851, when General Carrasco arrived in Sonora with a brigade of four hundred men.[101]   Carrasco boasted that he would exterminate the Indians on the Gila, but he died within a few months, and, aside from a few skirmishes with the Indians, no protection was given to the northern states.   Riddells, American consul at Chihuahua, declared that this military system of Mexico had failed to protect the Mexicans from the Indians.[102]   The whole system, he thought, was solely calculated, as the results showed, to annoy and molest American commerce on the frontier and to aid desertions from the American army.

Another Mexican plan was to induce Wild Cat and his band of three hundred Indian renegade warriors, Seminoles and Lipans, to abandon their American limits and to settle in Coahuila.[103]   Ten acres of land were given to each family, on condition that they protect the country from all other Indians.   Wild Cat soon interpreted this agreement as a license to make inroads across the Rio Grande into Texas.   Secretary Davis, in 1854, wrote that, ''scarcely a month passes without witnessing the butchery of some helpless family in Texas by savages from the West of the Bravo, who after the perpetration of their barbarities, recross the river and find shelter in the territories of the Mexican Republic.'' [104]

The Indian policy of the state of Texas further aided Indian incursions into Mexico.   By the terms of the compact by which Texas was admitted into the Union, she retained the ownership of all vacant lands within her limits,

101 *S. Ex. Docs.* (626), 32 Cong., 1 sess., XIV, no. 119, p. 412.

102 Riddells to Sec. of State, June 8, 1852, Dept. of State, Cons. Let., Chihuahua, vol. 1.

103 Smith to Webster, Feb. 16, 1851, Dept. of State, Des., Mex., vol. 15, no. 45.

104 Davis to Marcy, Dec. 29, 1854, Dept. of State, Misc. Let.

but the Indians became wards of the federal government.[105]
No portion of the state was assigned to the Indians, and as
fast as the settlements advanced, counties were formed and
the land was sold. This policy alarmed and irritated the
Indians and compelled them to resort to plunder for a
subsistence.[106] An attempt was made in the state legislature of 1851 to grant land to these tribes, but the only
legislation accomplished was to invest the governor with
the power to appoint a commissioner to confer upon this
subject with commissioners of the federal government.[107]

By 1853 Indian affairs in Texas had become a matter of
national importance. President Fillmore, in December,
1852, feared that unless Texas took some action to pacify
the Indians, the situation would become a serious embar-
rassment to the government.[108] Secretary Davis, September 19, 1853, notified Governor Bell, of Texas, that it
was impossible for the War Department to protect the
frontier in Texas, since the Indians could roam where
they wished and the military force could only interfere
when they assumed the character of an enemy.[109]

Furthermore, the American government was unable to
restrain its own citizens from participation in these Indian
inroads. Upon the frontier of Texas and New Mexico had
gathered a group of men of the worst description, who,
as Commissioner Bartlett said, "having no means of
support and being indisposed to labor, . . . obtained a livelihood by plundering both the Mexicans and
Americans."[110] Some people in New Mexico gained their

---

[105] *U. S. Statutes at Large*, V, 797–798.

[106] *S. Ex. Docs.* (658), 32 Cong., 2 sess., I, no. 1, p. 14.

[107] *Ibid.*, 435.

[108] *Ibid.*, 14.

[109] Davis to Bell, Sept. 19, 1853, *Journal of Texas House of Rep.*,
Fifth Leg., 1.

[110] *S. Ex. Docs.* (626), 32 Cong., 1 sess., XIV, no. 119, p. 441.

livelihood through the purchase of the articles stolen from
the Indians and the sale to the latter of arms and ammuni-
tion for their raids.[111]   In Texas, from 1851 to 1853,
Carvajal constantly led filibustering expeditions into the
Mexican territory, which attracted the lawless element to
the frontier.[112]   Secretary Webster informed Congress,
June 11, 1852, that if article XI was to be enforced, it was
necessary for the United States to restrain its own citizens
from hostile incursions into Mexico.[113]   He recommended
that Congress pass measures to enforce the American
neutrality laws.

Although the reports of devastation were always exaggerated by the Mexicans, the damage inflicted by these
Indian raids into Mexico was considerable.   Bonilla, Mexican Minister of Foreign Relations, in a description of the
Indian depredations in the northern states, complained of
"the assassination or captivity of all such persons as have
the misfortune of falling into their hands [the Indians]
without distinction of age or sex, the robbery and pillage of
herds of cattle and whatever property they meet with, the
desolation of villages and valuable plantations which are
laid waste and deserted and the continuous decay of such
states, once so flourishing, but now hardly able to sustain
themselves on account of their rapid depopulation and consequent abandonment of their agriculture, commerce, and
other sources of prosperity, owing entirely to this perpetual
cause of extermination."[114]   Of the town of Santa Cruz,
Sonora, Bartlett wrote that, "in such a miserable state of
existence were these people that they could scarcely ven-

[111] Letcher to Webster, Dec. 1, 1851, Dept. of State, Des., Mex.,
vol. 15, no. 10.

[112] *S. Ex. Docs.* (659), 32 Cong., 2 sess., II, no. 1, p. 16.

[113] *H. Ex. Docs.* (648), 32 Cong., 1 sess., XII, no. 112.

[114] Bonilla to Gadsden, Aug. 30, 1853, Dept. of State, Des., Mex.,
vol. 18, with no. 4.

ture beyond the walls of their town, except in parties of six or eight, who must be well armed."[115]   In Texas, in the year 1849, 204 persons were killed, wounded, or carried into captivity by the Indians, and property to the value of $103,277.00 was destroyed.[116]   In 1868, when the Mexican and American claims were adjusted, the Mexican government presented 366 claims for compensation, for losses and injuries inflicted by the American Indians from February 2, 1848, to December 30, 1853.   They made up an aggregate sum of $31,813,053.64⅝.[117]

The Mexican negotiators may have considered article XI a farce in 1848, but with the accumulation of these damages, the Mexican government demanded reparation by the United States.   Mexican claims began to pile up in the Department of State at Washington.   The Mexican minister, de la Rosa, in 1850, informed Secretary Clayton that the exact fulfillment of this article was the only advantage which Mexico derived from the treaty of Guadalupe Hidalgo.[118]   Ramírez, Mexican Minister of Foreign Relations, considered the enforcement of article XI, a small compensation for the loss of such valuable territory [119] Mexico began to use this breach of faith on the part of the United States as a rebuttal for all American claims against Mexico.   The slaughter and robbery of the Indians in the northern states became the most favored topic of the Mexican newspapers.[120]

Up to 1851 the American government had considered

[115] Bartlett, *Personal Narrative*, II, 407.

[116] *H. Reports* (584), 31 Cong., 1 sess., I, no. 280, p. 3.

[117] Moore, *Digest of International Arbitrations*, II, 1306.

[118] Rosa to Clayton, March 20, 1851, *H. Ex. Docs.* (577), 31 Cong., 1 sess., VIII, no. 62, p. 2.

[119] Ramírez to Letcher, Jan. 3, 1852, Dept. of State, Des., Mex., vol. 15, with no. 107.

[120] N. O. *Daily Picayune*, Sept. 13, 1853.

itself bound by article XI to indemnify Mexico for the Indian depredations. On November 10, 1849, Secretary Clayton admitted to Letcher that the obligations assumed by the United States in the treaty with Mexico were onerous. Great difficulty, he thought, would be experienced in the discharge of these duties.[121]  In the annual reports of the Departments of War and the Interior, the Secretaries emphasized the necessity for a strict fulfillment of these treaty obligations. Congressman R. W. Johnson, of Arkansas, declared in the House of Representatives, August 3, 1850 that "if we are bound to keep our Indians out of Mexico, we are liable for all damages caused by our neglect to do so." [122]  The House Committee on Indian Affairs reported, August 24, 1850, that article XI was a solemn treaty stipulation, and that neglect on the part of the United States to enforce it would result in claims against the government.[123]

When, however, Indian claims to the amount of millions of dollars were made the customary topic of correspondence of the Mexican minister, the government receded from Buchanan's view of America's duty and ability to fulfill the provisions. Furthermore, General Scott informed President Fillmore that an expenditure of $10,000,000 a year for ten or fifteen years was necessary to defend Mexico from the American Indians.[124]  Secretary Webster, in August, 1851, denied that the United States was bound to pay indemnity for Indian damages.[125]  He wrote

[121] Clayton to Letcher, Nov. 10, 1849, Dept. of State, Inst., Mex., vol. 16, no. 1.

[122] *Cong. Globe*, 31 Cong., 1 sess. (1849–50), XXI, pt. 2, p. 1516.

[123] *H. Reports* (584), 31 Cong., 1 sess., I, no. 280, p. 2.

[124] Fillmore to Webster, Aug. 17, 1851, *Pub. of Buffalo His. Soc.*, X, 350.

[125] Webster to Letcher, Aug. 19, 1851, Dept. of State, Inst., Mex., vol. 14, no. 72.

that "the United States cannot acquiesce in any construction of the treaty which would make that an absolute which must have been intended for a relative obligation." The United States, he argued, had restrained, prevented, and punished these Indians in the same manner as if their crimes had been committed against citizens of the United States.

Although he did not acknowledge the Mexican claims as lawful, Webster instructed Letcher, on August 19, 1851, to propose a convention to the Mexican government which would release the United States from any responsibility under article XI and thus free it of constant accusations of bad faith.[126] For the annulment of this article, Letcher was instructed to offer Mexico several million dollars, and the release from all accountability for American claims against Mexico since the treaty of Guadalupe Hidalgo. On February 2, 1852, Acting Secretary of State Derrick instructed Letcher to offer one or two million dollars in addition to the amount offered under former instructions.[127] Conkling, who succeeded Letcher in November, 1852, was instructed to make a similar offer for the release of article XI.[128]

The Mexican government, as usual, was badly in need of money, and it welcomed the suggestion of a release of article XI for a financial equivalent. It planned therefore, to make the most of the situation. Escandon, the official "money changer," was sent to Washington to ascertain how much the United States would actually give for such a release.[129] Although Letcher broached the subject to Ramírez in September, 1851, the latter refused

[126] *Ibid.*

[127] Derrick to Letcher, Feb. 27, 1852, *ibid.*, vol. 15, no. 87.

[128] Conrad to Conkling, Oct. 14, 1852, *ibid.*, vol. 16, no. 4.

[129] Letcher to Webster, Dec. 1, 1851, Dept. of State, Des., Mex., vol. 15, no. 100.

to consider it until his agent returned from Washington. Escandon returned in January, 1852, with the report that the United States would give at least $10,000,000 for the release of article XI.[130] De la Rosa, the Mexican minister at Washington, advised his government not to be so foolish as to make a treaty with the United States for any small amount.[131] According to Letcher, Escandon and other speculators, both Mexican and American, began to purchase Indian claims, which as Letcher said, "played the mischief with this business."[132] Letcher's offer of $2,000,000 and the payment of American claims against Mexico was disdainfully refused. The sum of $12,000,000 and the assumption of Mexican debts due to the United States was the least that Ramírez would accept.[133]

Conkling also attempted to get a release from this stipulation. Bonilla, a successor Ramírez, agreed to abrogate article XI, but he informed Conkling that an insignificant offer of eight to ten millions would be rejected by Mexico.[134] Bonilla declared that the Mexican government could reasonably insist on a sum of thirty-five to forty million dollars for the release, and that twenty millions was the very lowest sum that would be considered. The matter was then dropped and Conkling was shortly after recalled.

Thus article XI of the treaty of 1848 was the basis of a second issue with the Mexican government. The United States refused to accept the Mexican interpretation of the article, that a financial indemnity was due the Mexican citizens who suffered from the Indian depredations. On the other hand, Mexico rejected the pecuniary offer of the

[130] *Ibid.* to *ibid.*, Jan. 19, 1852, *ibid.*, vol. 15, private.
[131] *Ibid.* to *ibid.*, Jan. 24, 1852, *ibid.*
[132] *Ibid.*
[133] *Ibid.* to *ibid.*, Mar. 18, 1852, *ibid.*, vol. 15, no. 2.
[134] Conkling to Marcy, June 20, 1853, *ibid.*, vol. 17, no. 47.

American government for the abrogation of this article. While these negotiations were in progress, the Indian depredations continued and the claims for damages increased. American and Mexican speculators added another element to the situation. The Pierce administration which succeeded the Fillmore administration in 1853, and the new minister to Mexico, James Gadsden, had a difficult problem to solve.

# CHAPTER III

The importance of a road or canal across one of the isthmuses of Central America and Mexico was early recognized. Spanish explorers in the sixteenth century pointed out to their government the advantages of such a canal route.[1] The Spanish Cortes, by a decree of April 30, 1814, authorized the opening of a canal across the Isthmus of Tehuantepec, but the work was never undertaken.[2] The United States likewise was early interested in such an undertaking. The project was favored because it provided a safer and more direct trade route with Asia. Great Britain also was interested in such a road or canal.[3] With the development of steam locomotion, the plan of a railroad displaced the old idea of a road or canal, as a means of interoceanic connection.

The United States became vitally concerned in the construction of an isthmian connection when, by treaties of 1846 and 1848 with Great Britain and Mexico, she became owner of the entire Pacific Coast between modern Canada and Mexico. The discovery of gold in 1849 attracted thousands to California. In 1850 California was admitted

[1] Dallas, G. M., ''The Isthmus of Tehuantepec,'' in *Journal of the Franklin Institute,* Third series, XIV, 17.

[2] Garay, J. de., *An Account of the Isthmus of Tehuantepec,* 23.

[3] Williams, M. W., *Anglo-American Isthmian Diplomacy, 1815–1915.* This is the best work on the rivalry of the two nations for an isthmian route, but it is weak on the controversy over the Tehuantepec connection.

into the Union. The possession of an isthmian route was needed to insure quick intercourse between the eastern and the western parts of the nation. The Isthmus of Tehuantepec, which afforded the shortest and most suitable interoceanic connection for the United States, belonged to the Mexican Republic. It was in connection with this isthmian route that the third point of issue between the two governments arose.

Efforts were made to include the question of an isthmian route in the treaty negotiations with Mexico at the close of the Mexican War. Vice-President Dallas, in 1847, urged the securing of the Tehuantepec route from Mexico in the peace negotiations.[4] He thought that the sum of $20,000,000 could be expended out of the national treasury for such an acquisition. In the cabinet meetings when the instructions to the American negotiator were agreed upon, the Secretary of the Treasury, Robert J. Walker, considered the free passage across the Isthmus of Tehuantepec of more importance to the United States than the cession by Mexico of New Mexico and the Californias.[5] He insisted that the grant by Mexico of the free passage across the isthmus should be made a *sine qua non* in the making of any treaty. President Polk and the other members agreed that a free passage was important, but they would not go so far as Walker did.[6] Secretary of State, Buchanan, proposed that $5,000,000 of the sum paid Mexico should be expended by that country for the construction of a railroad or canal over the Isthmus of Tehuantepec, upon which the United States and its citizens could transport articles, free of custom duty.[7] The

[4] *Journal of the Franklin Inst.*, Third series, XIV, 20.

[5] Quaife, M. M., *Diary of James K. Polk*, II, 473.

[6] *Ibid.*

[7] ''Draft of article respecting the Isthmus of Tehuantepec as presented by me to the Cabinet,'' Buchanan Papers.

proposal of Buchanan was rejected by President Polk. In its place, Trist was authorized to offer $30,000,000 instead of $15,000,000 for New Mexico and Upper and Lower California if the right of transit across the Isthmus of Tehuantepec should be guaranteed to the United States.[8]

Trist was unable to include this demand in the treaty of Guadalupe Hidalgo. The Mexican negotiators refused to concede this privilege because British interests were involved. They informed Trist that such a grant had been made to a private contractor, but that the right of way was under the control of British subjects.[9] The matter was dropped by Trist in order to facilitate the adjustment of the boundary.[10]

Although the American commissioner was unable to secure this privilege in 1848, agitation for such a grant was continued by the American people. The length of the trip by the Isthmus of Panama, the extreme danger of a trip overland, and the doubt as to whether a transcontinental railroad could be built on American soil, all aided the plan for an isthmian route. Petitions were presented to Congress upon this subject. The Memphis Convention of 1849 recommended to the federal government the construction of a railroad across an isthmus in Central America as a means of increasing the facility of intercourse between the two oceans.[11] All agitation was put into tangible form in 1849 through the purchase of an isthmian grant by an American citizen.

On March 1, 1842, General Santa Anna, then President of Mexico, conceded to Don José de Garay the right of opening a communication between the Atlantic and

[8] *S. Ex. Docs.* (509), 30 Cong., 1 sess., VII, no. 52, p. 82.
[9] *Ibid.,* 337.
[10] Smith, *The War with Mexico,* II, 466.
[11] *De Bow's Commercial Review,* Mar. 1850 (VIII, 221).

Pacific Oceans, across the Isthmus of Tehuantepec.[12] This concession contained very liberal provisions for its holder. The Mexican government promised protection to the grantee and his assigns in the work, and permitted them to fix the tolls for fifty years on the canal or railway which they constructed. Important provisions were the grant to Garay of one hundred and fifty miles of land on both sides of the road or canal and the permission to colonize that region. All nations at peace with Mexico were to enjoy the advantages of this project. Construction of the road was to begin within two years after the completion of the preliminary survey.

Work on the project proceeded very slowly under the guidance of Garay. Santa Anna was removed from the presidency, but his successor, Bravo, recognized the Garay grant and extended every facility for the prosecution of the work.[13] In October, 1843, Santa Anna was restored to power, and as no progress had yet been made on the project, he extended the time for its commencement to July 1, 1845. In the winter of 1844, Santa Anna was again forced to abdicate, and was succeeded by a dictator, Mariano de Salas. Although the former extension of time had expired in July, 1846, Dictator Salas, in November, 1846, issued a decree extending Garay's time to November 5, 1848.[14] Because of these revolutionary periods and the Mexican War, Garay was unable to begin work.

Garay, also, it appears, had little thought of constructing the railroad or canal, as the grant had been a mere speculation on his part. Accordingly, in 1846, and 1848, he entered into several contracts with Messrs. Manning

[12] Ramírez, José F., *Memorias, negociaciones y documentos . . . por el istmo de Tehuantepec*, 4–9.

[13] *S. Reports* (631), 32 Cong., 1 sess., no. 355, p. 1.

[14] *Ibid.*, 2.

and Mackintosh, British subjects, for the sale of the grant.[15]  These contracts were formally consummated on September 28, 1848, and they also received the sanction of the Mexican government.  The possession of this grant by British subjects was the reason assigned by the Mexican negotiators for their refusal to consider the offer of the United States in 1847, for the purchase of a right of way across the Isthmus of Tehuantepec.  The purchase of the grant was also a speculation on the part of Manning and Mackintosh, and on February 5, 1849, they transferred their claim to P. A. Hargous, of New York City.[16] It is not known what sum Hargous paid for the grant, but it was rumored at the time to be only $25,000.[17]  At any rate, it was far below the figure of $3,500,000 which he later claimed for the loss of the grant.

P. A. Hargous and his two brothers, L. E. and L. S. Hargous, had been interested for many years in Mexican commercial and mercantile affairs.  They were originally citizens of Pennsylvania.  P. A. Hargous and Company or Hargous Brothers of New York City, as they were often called, owned a line of vessels plying between New York and Vera Cruz.  They transported merchandise for L. S. Hargous and Company of Vera Cruz, who conducted a large commission business in that city.[18]  This company was also a financial agent for both the American and Mexican governments.  It was the American agent for the collection of the annual installments of Mexican debt under the Claims convention of 1843.[19]  Trigueros, at one time Minister of Finance of Mexico, was also a partner in the L. S. Hargous Company, and through him, tran-

[15] *Ibid.*, 3.

[16] *S. Ex. Docs.* (621), 32 Cong., 1 sess., X, no. 97, p. 167.

[17] Butler, P., *Judah P. Benjamin*, 124.

[18] *S. Reports* (708), 33 Cong., 1 sess., II, pt. 2, no. 182, p. 55.

[19] *S. Reports* (808), 33 Cong., 2 sess., no. 142, p. 24.

sactions with the Mexican government were made.[20]   With P. A. Hargous as manager of the affairs in the United States and his brothers in charge of the business in Mexico, this combination carried on a series of speculations, from 1848 to 1861, which involved both the domestic and foreign policies of the American and Mexican governments.

On February 6, 1849, P. A. Hargous called the attention of congress to his grant.[21]   He pointed out the value of this concession to the United States, and asked the permission of Congress to present additional data before final congressional action was taken upon an isthmian route. He requested the Department of State to give governmental sanction to his concession.[22]   This, Secretary Clayton agreed to do.  He instructed Clifford to inform the Mexican government that the annulment of the grant, simply because it was in American hands, "would be regarded with just dissatisfaction by this Government."[23] An evasive answer was given by the Mexican government. It was denied that the American ownership of the grant would be the cause for such an act.[24]

Hargous was afraid to undertake the development of such a project without a guarantee of protection from both nations, and therefore, Secretary Clayton, in September, 1849, instructed Letcher to make a convention with Mexico, wherein both governments would promise protection to the work.[25]   Letcher accordingly negotiated

[20] *S. Reports* (708), 33 Cong., 1 sess., II, pt. 2, no. 182, p. 48.

[21] *S. Misc. Docs.* (533), 30 Cong., 2 sess., I, no. 50.

[22] Hargous to Clayton, Feb. 16, 1850, *S. Ex. Docs.* (621), 32 Cong., 1 sess., X, no. 97, p. 15.

[23] Clayton to Clifford, Apr. 30, 1849, Dept. of State, Inst., Mex., vol. 16, no. 19.

[24] Lacunza to Clifford, July 11, 1849, *S. Ex. Docs.* (621), 32 Cong., 1 sess., X, no. 97, p. 10.

[25] Clayton to Letcher, Sept. 18, 1849, Dept. of State, Inst., Mex., vol. 16, no. 1.

a convention with Mexico, June 22, 1850, for a reciprocal guarantee of protection to the undertaking, but it in fact gave little guarantee, as the United States could interfere to protect the grantee only when summoned by the Mexican government.[26] Opposition by the Mexican people to any convention was so strong that Letcher informed Clayton that the convention negotiated "was neck or nothing."[27] Article XII of the convention stated that the assent of P. A. Hargous was necessary before it could be ratified.

Before the convention was negotiated, P. A. Hargous had made an arrangement with a number of citizens in New Orleans for the development of his concession. New Orleans was interested in an isthmian route because it would benefit more from that improvement than would any other city in the United States. The New Orleans *Bulletin* stated in 1848 that "the commercial destiny of New Orleans can never be completed until a regular water communication is established between the Gulf of Mexico and the Pacific."[28] Judah P. Benjamin declared in 1852 that when the route was completed, "the whole trade of the East must almost of a necessity pass through New Orleans."[29] Thus when Hargous offered his concession to New Orleans, it was immediately accepted by prominent and enterprising citizens, under the leadership of Judah P. Benjamin. A temporary agreement was made between Hargous and this group for the formation of a corporation with a capital of $9,000,000, in which Hargous received one third interest for the sale of his con-

---

[26] Letcher to Clayton, June 24, 1850, Dept. of State, Des., Mex., vol. 14, no. 29.

[27] *Ibid.* to *ibid.*, June 24, 1850, Clayton Papers, vol. 9.

[28] Washington *Union*, Dec. 13, 1848.

[29] *De Bow's Review*, May 1852 (XII, 564).

cession.[30] This New Orleans Company, or the Tehuantepec Railroad Company, as it was often called, was never
incorporated, but a temporary organization was formed
with Judah P. Benjamin as chairman and Bernard Fallon
as secretary.[31] A survey of the route was at once begun
by this company, consent for which was granted by the
Mexican government.[32] The sum of $245,000 was expended
by the company on the survey.[33] The report of Engineer
Barnard justified all the former statements as to the
availability of this route for an interoceanic connection.[34]

Secretary Webster considered the convention of June,
1850, as sufficient protection to Hargous, and he demanded
the assent of Hargous to it.[35] Hargous refused to accept
this agreement and he advised Webster to obtain several
amendments to the convention.[36] This Webster agreed to
do, and Letcher was instructed, on August 24, 1850, to
make such alterations in the convention as would expressly
protect the grant.[37] Webster's amendments were rejected
by the Mexican government, and as negotiations were about
to fail, Webster, on the advice of Hargous, directed Letcher
to secure "a treaty as favorable as practicable for the
interests of the United States and the holders of the
grant."[38] A convention was accordingly made on Jan-

[30] *S. Ex. Docs.* (621), 32 Cong., 1 sess., X, no. 97, p. 127.

[31] Butler, *Judah P. Benjamin,* 125.

[32] Letcher to Webster, Oct. 29, 1851, Dept. of State, Des., Mex., vol. 14, no. 97.

[33] Sumner to Marcy, June 2, 1854, Dept. of State, Misc. Let.

[34] *De Bow's Review,* July 1852 (XIII, 45).

[35] Webster to Hargous, Aug. 13, 1850, *S. Ex. Docs.* (621), 32 Cong., 1 sess., X, no. 97, p. 26.

[36] Hargous to Webster, Aug. 26, 1850, *ibid.,* 28.

[37] Webster to Letcher, Aug. 24, 1850, Dept. of State, Inst., Mex., vol. 16, no. 42.

[38] *Ibid.* to *ibid.,* Dec. 4, 1850, *ibid.,* vol. 16, no. 47.

uary 21, 1851, by Letcher, which contained principles, in the main, favorable to Hargous and his associates.[39]

In the meantime, public sentiment in Mexico had turned against the Garay grant. This was due mainly to Mexican fear of the plans of the New Orleans Company. By the Garay grant, one hundred and fifty miles of territory on both sides of the route were given to the holder of the grant. The New Orleans Company intended to make use of this concession. Beautiful pictures were painted of the development of the isthmus, lands were offered for sale, and colonization was invited there. Such actions, Rosa complained to Webster, were insults to his government.[40] Buckingham Smith, minister *ad interim*, in Mexico, informed Webster that the grant was condemned by all parties, and that all used the common argument, that "the' experiment with Texas should be enough; and to give our neighbors a foothold in Tehuantepec will certainly end in the seizure of one-half the remaining territory of the Republic."[41]

To annul the original grant was the easiest way to stop the operations of the New Orleans Company, and Mexico proceeded to do this. A committee was appointed in the Mexican Senate to consider the Tehuantepec question. On March 24, 1851, it recommended that the grant be declared null, because the provisional government had no authority to issue the decree of November 5, 1846, which extended the time of Garay's contract.[42] The Senate by a vote of

[39] *S. Ex. Docs.* (621), 32 Cong., 1 sess., X, no. 97, pp. 47–50.

[40] Rosa to Webster, Mar. 1, 1851, Dept. of State, Notes to Dept., Mex. Leg., vol. 7.

[41] Smith to Webster, Apr. 1, 1851, Dept. of State, Des., Mex., vol. 14, no. 49.

[42] *El Universal*, Apr. 10–15, 1851.

34 to 7 agreed to the report.[43]  The House of Deputies by a vote of 60 to 10 accepted the Senate bill, and on May 22, 1851, President Arista published a decree which declared the Garay grant to be null and void.[44]  Rosa explained to Webster that the grant was declared null in order to stop the contemptuous remarks and insults aimed at the Mexican government by a mere corporation, and to prevent "the emigration of adventurers from every part of the world toward that point of the republic." [45]

In addition to the annulment of the grant, the Mexican government took steps to halt the work of the New Orleans Company.  President Arista ordered the governor of Oajaca to stop all surveys in that region.[46]  Four military colonies were established on the isthmus in order to enforce the decree.[47]  Laborers for the company were not permitted to land at the isthmus,[48] and barges of the company were seized by Mexican officials.[49]  The exequatur of C. R. Webster, the American consul at Tehuantepec, was temporarily withdrawn.[50]  In reply to the threat of the New Orleans Company that it would continue to carry on the enterprise, the Mexican Minister of Foreign Relations declared that any such attempt would be repelled and punished, and if force were introduced, the Mexican government

[43] Smith to Webster, Apr. 14, 1851, Dept. of State, Des., Mex., vol. 14, no. 52.

[44] Ibid. to ibid., June 4, 1851, ibid., vol. 14, no. 61.

[45] Rosa to Webster, July 3, 1851, Dept. of State, Notes to Dept., Mex. Leg., vol. 7.

[46] Smith to Webster, June 28, 1851, Dept. of State, Des., Mex., vol. 14, no. 70.

[47] Ibid. to ibid., Aug. 2, 1851, ibid., vol. 14, no. 78.

[48] Ibid. to ibid., June 28, 1851, ibid., vol. 14, no. 70.

[49] Hargous to Webster, Oct. 15, 1851, S. Ex. Docs. (621), 32 Cong., 1 sess., X, no. 97, p. 98.

[50] Derrick to Letcher, Sept. 10, 1851, Dept. of State, Inst., Mex., vol. 16, no. 75.

would be compelled "to treat said Company's agents with all the severity which the laws of nations authorized." [51]

The convention of January 25, 1851, was accepted by P. A. Hargous, and Secretary Webster returned it to Mexico for ratification in the midst of the congressional proceedings on the Garay grant. With the annulment of the grant, opposition to the convention became more violent. The opposition came from every quarter in Mexico. Letcher wrote, "Damn the treaty; it's opposed by all the foreign influence, by the opposition party, and by all the moneyed and commercial men of this country in solid column." [52] Later he declared that it was opposed, "by the clergy, by the President, by both Houses of Congress, by every political party, by every faction and fragment in the whole country." [53] Smith informed Webster that the people of the country had but one mind on the subject, and that no Congress would ever ratify the Tehuantepec convention.[54] Mexico was determined to stand a war rather than agree to the convention.[55]

There was also a strong outside opposition to the convention. Foreign influence was opposed to the ratification.[56] Speculators in America who held Mexican grants for other routes were loath to see a monopolization of the whole business by Hargous. Citizens of New York and Washington wrote letters to President Arista, members of Congress,

[51] Ramírez to Letcher, Dec. 13, 1851, Dept. of State, Des., Mex., vol. 15, with no. 101.

[52] Letcher to Crittenden, Oct. 20, 1850, Coleman, C., *Life of John J. Crittenden,* I, 383.

[53] Letcher to Webster, Oct. 29, 1851, Dept. of State, Des., Mex., vol. 14, no. 97.

[54] Smith to Webster, Sept. 14, 1851, *ibid.,* vol. 14, no. 85.

[55] Letcher to Crittenden, Dec. 1851, Crittenden Papers, vol. 10.

[56] Letcher to Webster, Jan. 17, 1851, Dept. of State, Des., Mex., vol. 14, no. 43.

and private individuals of Mexico, in which they advised rejection of the convention.[57]

American newspapers, hostile to the convention, were sent to Mexico. Such propaganda on the part of American citizens weakened Letcher's efforts for the ratification of the convention. In a protest to Webster, he declared that he had expected foreign opposition but said that "a fire from the rear, took me by surprise."[58] The American government took cognizance of these illegal acts of American citizens in holding correspondence with a foreign power, with the intent to influence its relations with the United States. Jonas P. Levy, holder of a Mexican railroad grant, was prosecuted, under the act of January 30, 1799, for his attempt to influence President Arista's attitude to the convention.[59] Thus, with both interior and exterior hostile interests, the Tehuantepec convention had little chance of ratification by the Mexican government.

The Mexican Congress opposed the convention more violently than did President Arista, and that body took the initiative in the fight against ratification. On August 2, 1851, the Senate called upon the Minister of Foreign Relations for a report on the status of the matter.[60] In order to delay rejection of the convention, Letcher agreed with Ramírez to reopen negotiations, and the convention was not sent to the Senate.[61] For having reopened the matter with Letcher the Minister of Foreign Relations was publicly reprimanded by the Senate.[62] The next move of Letcher was to induce Ramírez to postpone the presen-

---

[57] *Ibid.* to *ibid.*, Dec. 14, 1851, *ibid.*, vol. 15, no. 101.

[58] *Ibid.*

[59] Charleston *Daily Courier*, Feb. 9, 1852.

[60] Smith to Webster, Aug. 2, 1851, Dept. of State, Des., Mex., vol. 14, no. 78.

[61] Letcher to Webster, Oct. 29, 1851, *ibid.*, vol. 14, no. 97.

[62] *Ibid.*

tation of the convention to Congress until April 8, 1852, as he believed a revolution in Mexico was near at hand, and with the change of government, he thought the convention would be ratified.[63]   At Letcher's suggestion, President Fillmore wrote a firm letter to President Arista, in which he threatened that if the convention were rejected, it would disturb the harmonious relations of the two governments.[64]   Letcher's diplomacy was ineffective, for when the convention was presented to the Chamber of Deputies, it was immediately rejected by a vote of 71 to 1.[65] The opposition was so strong that members with a direct interest in the grant voted against the convention.[66] With the Garay grant annuled and the Tehuantepec convention rejected, it appeared as if American influence in the isthmus was at an end.

Mexico, however, regardless of her boastings, feared the consequences of her action.  While it refused to accept the Garay grant, the Mexican government repeatedly asserted that it was willing to grant such privileges to the United States upon almost any other terms.  Ramírez declared to Letcher, "Leave out the Garay grant, say nothing about it, and I am ready to enter into a treaty with you, which I think will be satisfactory to both countries." [67]   Ramírez presented Letcher with a counter-proposal for an isthmian connection, by which the railroad or canal was to be constructed by a private company under the protection of Mexico and those governments, both American and European, which agreed to the plan.  This proposal, however,

[63] *Ibid.* to *ibid.*, Jan. 24, 1852, *ibid.*, vol. 15, private.

[64] Fillmore to Arista, Mar. 19, 1852, *S. Ex. Docs.* (621), 32 Cong., 1 sess., X, no. 97, p. 168.

[65] Letcher to Webster, Apr. 8, 1852, Dept. of State, Des., Mex., vol. 15, no. 4.

[66] *Ibid.*

[67] *Ibid.* to *ibid.*, Dec. 14, 1851, *ibid.*, vol. 15, no. 101.

was characterized by Letcher as "a child of three fathers, a Mexican, a Spaniard, and an Englishman."[68]  Later the Mexican government offered to treat with the New Orleans Company for a new grant, if all pretensions to the Garay claim were abandoned.[69]  All these proposals Letcher refused to accept, as his government still maintained the validity of the Garay grant.

The rejection of the Tehuantepec convention by Mexico, forced the American government to make the next move. The New Orleans Company was determined that the government should take some action. Hargous solemnly protested against the action of Mexico and presented to the Department of State a claim of $5,283,000 against that government.[70]  He demanded that the administration enforce the contract of the grantees with Mexico. Judah P. Benjamin personally informed President Fillmore that the company intended to insist upon the validity of their grant and would send men to prosecute the work, so that a collision with Mexico would compel the administration "to sustain its own citizens . . . or unite with Mexico in punishing them."[71]  As a result, the administration was compelled either to protect the grant or to recede from its former threats and assertions.

Webster had constantly warned Mexico of the consequences which would follow rejection of the grant and the convention. Letcher was instructed in December, 1851, to inform the Mexican government that if the convention were not ratified, very serious consequences would result.[72]

[68] *Ibid.* to *ibid.*, Jan. 4, 1852, *ibid.*, vol. 15, no. 103.

[69] Arista to Fillmore, Apr. 15, 1852, *S. Ex. Docs.* (621), 32 Cong., 1 sess., X, no. 97, p. 160.

[70] Hargous to Webster, May 31, 1852; June 5, 1852, *ibid.*, 149–150.

[71] Fillmore to Webster, July 19, 1851, Webster Papers, vol. 10.

[72] Webster to Letcher, Dec. 23, 1851, Crittenden Papers, vol. 16.

Gonzales de la Vega, Mexican minister *ad interim* was informed on March 15, 1852, that the American government was determined to "bring these embarrassing and painful questions to a conclusion," and therefore an ultimate decision of Mexico was demanded.[73] These were only threats, however, for the administration was not willing to resort to arms to protect a private corporation.

President Fillmore considered the project an important national undertaking and desired to protect the grant, if it could be peaceably accomplished. But as he informed Webster, he would not "see the nation involved in a war with Mexico to gratify the wishes or cupidity of any private company."[74] Again, he informed Webster that "the rights of the company like every other contractor with a foreign country, are rights growing out of a private contract; the proprietors doubtless have a pecuniary indemnity, but that is to be settled like every other claim of this kind, that our citizens may have against a foreign government."[75]

The Garay grant had been so strongly supported by the administration because of another reason. The fear that a European nation, especially, Great Britain, might acquire the Tehuantepec route had been the main factor in the aggressive policy of the administration. This fact is shown in the correspondence of the Department of State. Letcher was ordered to include an article in the Tehuantepec convention whereby no foreign government or corporation was eligible to purchase the Garay grant.[76] Webster informed Larrainzar in 1852 that the United States would never allow a communication to be placed under the exclusive

[73] Webster to Gonzales de la Vega, Mar. 15, 1852, Dept. of State, Notes from Dept., Mex. Leg., vol. 6.
[74] Fillmore to Webster, July 19, 1851, Webster Papers, vol. 10.
[75] *Ibid.* to *ibid.*, May 20, 1852, Van Tyne, C. H., *The Letters of Daniel Webster*, 528.

supervision of a third party.[77]   President Fillmore was certain that the British minister in Mexico was using his means to defeat the Garay grant and the Tehuantepec convention.[78]   A proposition offered in the Mexican Senate to cede the Tehuantepec route to Great Britain aroused the ire of both government and citizens of the United States. Webster informed Letcher that the United States would never allow the grant to pass into the hands of any European power, and that the news of such negotiations, "produced in America impressions very unfavorable to Mexico." [79]

The fears of the administration were unfounded for Great Britain during this period was interested in isthmian routes farther south.[80]   Also, after the Clayton-Bulwer treaty, the former aggressive isthmian policy of Great Britain was considerably moderated.   Although the American ministers to Mexico reported evidences of foreign influence, no definite step was taken by the British government or British individuals to acquire the Tehuantepec route.   But, the fear of such a move shaped Webster's isthmian policy.

After the rejection of the Tehuantepec convention, no further action was taken by the administration to bring the matter to a conclusion.   After the death of Webster in October, 1852, the tone of the correspondence from the Department of State was more moderate.   Conrad, Acting Secretary of State, informed Conkling that "the United States could not with a due regard to its own dignity make

[76] Clayton to Letcher, Sept. 18, 1849, Dept. of State, Inst., Mex., vol. 16, no. 1.

[77] Webster to Larrainzar, June 30, 1852, S. Ex. Docs. (621), 32 Cong., 1 sess., X, no. 97, p. 152.

[78] Fillmore to Webster, July 19, 1851, Webster Papers, vol. 10.

[79] Webster to Letcher, Dec. 22, 1851, Dept. of State, Inst., Mex., vol. 16, no. 79.

[80] Williams, Anglo-American Isthmian Diplomacy, 67–195.

any overtures to renew the negotiations." [81] Conrad thought that the next move must come from Mexico, and accordingly Conkling was ordered to consider any proposition offered by Mexico, but at the same time to have the Garay grant connected with it.[82] In July, 1852, all the correspondence was sent to the Senate and President Fillmore washed his hands of the whole affair. Secretary Everett informed Larrainzar in January, 1853, that not until there was peace in Mexico and the Garay grant was satisfactorily adjusted by the Mexican government, would the United States consider negotiations to solve the isthmian question.[83]

The United States Senate refused to accept the conciliatory policy of the administration. On August 30, 1852, the Committee on Foreign Relations reported a series of resolutions on the subject.[84] It was declared incompatible with the dignity of the nation to negotiate further with Mexico. Asserting that it was the duty of the government to protect its citizens at home or abroad, the committee declared that unless Mexico at once reconsidered her decision, it was the duty of the United States "to adopt such measures as will preserve the honor of the country and the rights of the citizens." [85] Senator Mason, of Virginia, was of the opinion that "if the transit be considered as indispensable to our welfare, it must be conceded or it will be taken by strong hand." [86] Intervention in Mexico to sustain the grant was urged by Senators Downs, of

[81] Conrad to Conkling, Oct. 14, 1852, Dept. of State, Inst., Mex., vol. 17, no. 4.

[82] *Ibid.*

[83] Everett to Larrainzar, Jan. 31, 1853, Dept. of State, Notes from Dept., Mex. Leg., vol. 6.

[84] *S. Reports* (631), 32 Cong., 1 sess., II, no. 355, pp. 1–20.

[85] *Ibid.*, 6.

[86] *Cong. Globe*, 32 Cong., 2 sess. (1852–53), XXVII, App., 138.

Louisiana, and Brooks, of Mississippi.[87]   Seward, of New York, and Hale, of New Hampshire, however, argued that the United States had no reason to protect a mere corporation.[88]   The session closed on March 3, 1853, without any definite action by the Senate on the matter.   Meanwhile, in Mexico the whole subject was further complicated through another isthmian grant by the Mexican government.

The Mexican government had asserted continuously that it would consider any isthmian proposal not connected with the Garay grant.   This, with the fear of American reprisals and the generous use of money by American speculators, produced another isthmian grant.   On May 14, 1852, one month after the rejection of the Tehuantepec convention, a bill was passed by the Mexican Congress which invested the President with power to open a communication between the Atlantic and Pacific Oceans.[89]   On July 29, 1852, the "Bases" for such a work were published by the chief executive and proposals for the concession were invited.[90]

When Congress met in special session, in October, 1852, it assumed control of the whole matter.   A scramble for the concession was made by five companies, three of which were controlled by American citizens.   P. A. Hargous reappeared on the scene, and made an offer for the concession through his agent, Alexander Bellangé.[91]   His greatest competitor was A. G. Sloo, who was represented by W. D. Lee, an attaché of the American legation.   On November 16, 1852, the committee of the Chamber of

[87] *Ibid.*, 138–140; 165–170.

[88] *Ibid.*, 140–147; 160–165.

[89] Letcher to Webster, May 5, 1852, Dept. of State, Des., Mex., vol. 15, no. 7.

[90] *Ibid.* to *ibid.*, Aug. 1, 1852, *ibid.*, vol. 15, no. 19.

[91] *Documentos relativos a la apertura . . . por el istmo de Tehuantepec*, 38–45.

Deputies after a consideration of the proposals recommended the acceptance of the offer of Bellangé.[92] An investigation, however, proved that this company had previously seen the offers of the other companies, so new proposals were invited.[93] Thus so nearly had P. A. Hargous come into possession of another isthmian concession. Bribery was the common practice of all companies. Conkling wrote that "of the means resorted to, and it is said openly invited by the Deputies, to obtain votes, I abstain from speaking."[94] The resignation of President Arista halted congressional action on the Tehuantepec question.

President Arista, as already noted, chose to retire quietly before a rising storm of revolution and therefore abdicated his office on January 5, 1852.[95] Out of eighteen aspirants for the office, Juan Ceballos, President of the Supreme Court was chosen President *ad interim* by the Chamber of Deputies.[96] In order to restore order in the nation, Ceballos was given extraordinary powers by Congress on January 11, 1853. When Congress dared to take issue with Ceballos on the revision of the constitution, he drove out the legislators with bayonets and closed the chambers.[97] Before the dissolution of Congress, he had withdrawn the Tehuantepec subject from that body, as he considered it to be an executive question.[98]

A. G. Sloo, who since the annulment of the Garay grant had endeavored to get an isthmian grant, was now successful in his endeavors. On February 5, 1853, the day before

[92] Rich to Webster, Nov. 20, 1852, Dept. of State, Des., Mex., vol. 15, no. 25.
[93] Conkling to Webster, Nov. 23, 1852, *ibid.*, vol. 16, no. 1.
[94] *Ibid.*
[95] Conkling to Everett, Jan. 7, 1853, *ibid.*, vol. 16, no. 12.
[96] *Ibid.*
[97] *Ibid.* to *ibid.*, Feb. 2, 1852, *ibid.*, vol. 16, no. 14.
[98] Lee to Marcy, Mar. 28, 1853, Dept. of State, Misc. Let.

he was forced to abdicate, President Ceballos, issued a
decree by which Sloo was invested with the power to
open a communication through the Isthmus of Tehuantepec.[99] All the objectionable features of the Garay grant
were eliminated. No colonization was permissible; no
armed forces were to be transported; foreigners who held
stock in the enterprise were to be responsible to the Mexican laws; and no foreign government could become a
partner in the work. For this concession, Sloo was to pay
$600,000, of which $300,000 was due on the day the contract was signed.

Sloo was an American soldier of fortune. He was a
native of Kentucky, but had spent most of his life in the
northern states.[100] He had on several occasions received
mail contracts from the American government to transport mail from New York to Havana, but he always reas-
signed these contracts to others.[101] As he was not a man of
means, this Mexican move on his part was only a bold
adventure. In order to make the first payment to the
Mexican government, Sloo was forced in consideration of
a loan to hypothecate the grant to F. P. Falconet, a British
banker.[102] The agreement was that if the notes were not
paid at maturity, the grant should then revert to Falconet,
without any judicial or other proceedings.[103]

Sloo went at once to New Orleans where he formed the
Tehuantepec Company, which was chartered March 12,
1853, under the laws of the State of Louisiana.[104] The
capital of the corporation was fixed at $10,000,000. One

[99] Washington *Daily National Intelligencer*, Mar. 9, 1853.

[100] *S. Reports* (891), 34 Cong., 3 sess., I, no. 440.

[101] *S. Ex. Docs.* (692), 33 Cong., 1 sess., III, no. 1, p. 725.

[102] *U. S. and Mex. Claims Commission, 1868*, Dept. of State,
Opinions, III, no. 57.

[103] *Ibid.*

[104] N. O. *Daily Picayune*, July 2, 1853.

half of the stock of the company was held by Sloo and his assigns, for the sale of the concession.

The operations of the company began with a flourish. In March, 1853, formal possession was taken of the isthmus.[105]  James Sykes and Company, of England, were engaged to build the railroad.[106]  In October, 1853, Sloo made a proposal to the American government to carry the mail between New Orleans and San Francisco over the Tehuantepec route.[107]  He promised to transport mail from New York to San Francisco in fifteen days less time than was possible over all other routes and to be ready to undertake the work by January 1, 1855. All of these plans were spoiled when in a short time, Sloo was unable to meet his obligations to Falconet. The latter, then, in control of the grant, transfered it to P. A. Hargous, and thus, by April 16, 1855, Hargous and his New Orleans group owned both the Garay and the Sloo grants.[108]

Conkling's diplomacy was influenced by W. D. Lee, an attaché of the American legation.  After Lee had purchased the isthmian grant for Sloo, he advised Conkling to make a treaty with Mexico, whereby both governments should recognize the Sloo grant and promise it protection.[109] Conkling agreed to this suggestion and at once demanded instructions from his government upon the subject.[110]  He informed Everett that a glorious opportunity to secure an isthmian route might be lost by delay.[111]

[105] Webster to Marcy, May 17, 1853, Dept. of State, Cons. Let., Tehuantepec, vol. 1.

[106] N. O. *Daily Picayune*, Oct. 11, 1853.

[107] *S. Ex. Docs.* (692), 33 Cong., 1 sess., III, no. 1, p. 169.

[108] *U. S. and Mex. Claims Commissions, 1868*, Dept. of State, Opinions, III, no. 57.

[109] Conkling to Sec. of State, Mar. 24, 1853, Dept. of State, Des., Mex., vol. 16, no. 26.

[110] Conkling to Everett, Feb. 2, 1853, *ibid.*, vol. 16, no. 14.

[111] *Ibid.* to *ibid.*, Feb. 6, 1853, *ibid.*, vol. 16, no. 18.

No instructions were sent by the retiring administration, and Conkling without any advice from the new administration, signed on March 21, 1853, a convention by which Mexico and the United States agreed jointly to protect the Sloo grant.[112] Conkling did this under the impression that since he was unable to get recognition for the Garay grant, he still had the Tehuantepec route in American hands and under American protection. Lee, rather than Conkling, negotiated the convention, for, as Conkling wrote, "Lee broke down all jealousies and impediments." [113] The current speculation of that time had entered into the American legation in Mexico.

Thus the isthmian question with its tangled threads had involved the diplomatic relations of the two governments. The Garay grant had been annulled by the Mexican government, but the grantees still maintained its validity. They demanded either armed intervention by the American government in Mexico to protect their rights or a large indemnity from Mexico for the losses sustained. The Sloo grant further complicated matters, because a convention had been made by an American minister, which bound the American government to protect this grant. The outcome depended upon the decision of the new administration in the United States. If the Sloo grant were accepted, then the former policy of the nation in favor of the Garay grant would be repudiated. The holders of each concession were determined to have their respective grants favored by the incoming administration, and were unconcerned as to the means to be used for this purpose.

The boundary dispute with its appendage, the transcontinental railroad matter; the issue arising from Indian depredations in Mexico, and the isthmian question were the

[112] Conkling to Sec. of State, Mar. 24, 1853, *ibid.*, vol. 16, no. 26.
[113] *Ibid.*

antecedents of the Gadsden treaty.  In addition, there were other minor quarrels between the two nations, occasioned by commercial disputes, tariff controversies, and the expeditions of filibusters, but these were insignificant when compared with the three main issues.  Franklin Pierce, when he became President, March 4, 1853, had either to negotiate with Mexico to relieve all these issues or to allow them to continue until settled by force.  He chose the former method and the result of his program was the Gadsden treaty.

# CHAPTER IV

## THE NEGOTIATION OF THE GADSDEN TREATY

In November, 1852, the Democratic party, with a comparatively unknown standard bearer, triumphed over the Whig party. The Democratic platform pledged the party to a faithful execution of the compromise measures of 1850, including the Fugitive Slave Law, and promised to resist all attempts to renew the slavery question.[1] The Democratic party was outwardly united, while the Whig party was more deeply split into the northern and southern groups, as the slavery question had made it impossible for such leaders as Toombs and Seward to meet on common ground.[2] The Whig platform was not so definite on the Compromise measures of 1850, and the nomination of General Winfield Scott, a man of Free-Soil tendencies, not pledged to the finality of the Compromise of 1850, further divided the party.[3]

The campaign of the summer and fall of 1852 was characterized by its lack of public interest. As both parties were pledged in their platforms to maintain the compromise acts of 1850, the personal antecedents and views of the candidates became the real issue in the campaign. The election resulted in a landslide for the Democratic candidate, Franklin Pierce, who received 254 electoral votes to

[1] Stanwood, E., *A History of the Presidency*, 249.
[2] Smith, T. C., *Parties and Slavery*, 34.
[3] *Ibid.*, 36.

42 for Scott and carried every state except Massachusetts, Vermont, Kentucky, and Tennessee.[4]

Pierce had been nominated, not so much because he was the choice of a majority of the Democratic party, but because the delegates at the Baltimore convention were unable to agree upon any of the leading candidates for the Democratic nomination. The selection of Pierce came as a result of a skillfully conducted campaign on the part of certain leaders, and because it was believed that a man of less decided position on national issues than the old line candidates would have a better opportunity to win. It was not however, until the forty-ninth ballot, when the impossibility of the nomination of Buchanan, Cass, Douglas, or Marcy was realized, that the stampede to Pierce occurred. The qualifications of Pierce were, as his campaign biographer wrote, "personal attractions and no record to attack and no enemies to fear."[5] Pierce cannot be classed as a great statesman; nor did he ever show great qualities as a leader. He has been described as "simply a man of moderate abilities, good intentions, and personally attractive qualities, who was wholly dominated by his party and its acknowledged leaders."[6]

All elements of the Democratic party and all sections of the country were represented in Pierce's cabinet. A newspaper which commented favorably upon the selection, declared, "Cushing represents New England; Marcy, the great Commercial Center of America; Campbell, the Conservative Middle; Dobbin, the Union-loving South; Davis, the extreme and fiery South; Guthrie, the Southwest, and McClelland, that growing arm of the Confederacy—the states of the Northwest."[7] The cabinet was divided over

---

[4] Stanwood, *A History of the Presidency*, 257.

[5] Hawthorne, N., *Franklin Pierce*, 109.

[6] Smith, *Parties and Slavery*, 97.

[7] *Daily Wisconsin*, Mar. 6, 1853, with Marcy Papers, vol. 31.

the slavery question. Marcy had been the leader of the New York Hunkers, but McClelland had been an active anti-slavery man; Guthrie and Dobbin were conservative southern Democrats, while Davis was the leader of the State Rights Democrats.[8] With these divergent elements in the cabinet, it was predicted that a split would soon occur, but this cabinet had the unique distinction of serving throughout the entire administration without a single change.

The selection of W. L. Marcy as Secretary of State was a shrewd effort on the part of Pierce to meet the exigencies of New York politics. On the whole, Marcy truly deserved the title since given to him of "A Great Secretary of State."[9] He was an extremely busy Secretary of State. He informed John Y. Mason, on one occasion, that he had twenty treaties on his hands.[10] Again, on the same date, he wrote Mason, "If you knew the pressure of business upon me, you would not expect private letters nor a large amount of public despatches."[11] It is no surprise then, that the dispatches of the American ministers often remained unanswered.

Although he was a northern man, Pierce was dominated by the southern wing of the Democratic party. He admitted to Duff Green that he was indebted to the state rights section of the party for his nomination and election.[12] He was particularly under the influence of Jefferson Davis, Secretary of War. Immediately after his election, Pierce invited Davis to come North, in order that he

[8] Rhodes, J. F., *History of the United States from Compromise of* 1850, I, 388.

[9] Moore, J. B., "A Great Secretary of State," in *Pol. Science Quar.*, XXX, 371.

[10] Marcy to Mason, May 25, 1854, Marcy Papers, vol. 50.

[11] *Ibid.* to *ibid.*, May 25, 1854, *ibid.*, Private letter-book.

[12] Green to Marcy, Aug. 12, 1853, Marcy Papers, vol. 41.

might as he wrote, "converse with you of the South and particularly of my Cabinet."[13] Colonel T. C. Greene, of Boston, was designated as the medium of correspondence. Davis was unable to visit Pierce but considerable correspondence ensued.[14] So great was the desire of Pierce to see Davis that telegrams were sent to the latter, which urged him to come to Washington by February 15, 1853.[15] Davis was unable to reach Washington by that date, and this caused Greene again to wire him to come as soon as possible.[16] This intimacy was continued throughout the entire administration, and although Marcy and Cushing were forceful members of the Cabinet, the primary influence over Pierce rested with Davis.[17] This influence was shown in the appointment of ministers to foreign countries, as Davis had urged the selection of Soulé, John Y. Mason and others.[18] At the end of his term of office, Pierce said to Davis, "I can scarcely bear the parting from you, who have been strength and solace to me for four anxious years and never failed me."[19]

President Pierce entered upon his duties with the intention of making permanent the Compromise measures of 1850, and thus to secure domestic tranquility in the United States. This program however was soon demolished through the introduction by Stephen A. Douglas of the Kansas-Nebraska bill into the Senate. This bill, the North declared, destroyed the Compromise of 1850, and the con-

[13] Pierce to Davis, Dec. 7, 1852, Pierce Papers, vol. 4.

[14] *Ibid.* to *ibid.*, Jan. 12, 1853, *ibid.*

[15] Greene to Davis, Feb. 2, 1853, *ibid.*

[16] Davis to Greene, Feb. 13, 1853; Greene to Davis, Feb. 18, 1853, *ibid.*

[17] Dodd, W. E., *Jefferson Davis*, 137.

[18] *Ibid.*

[19] Davis, V. J., *Jefferson Davis, Ex-President of the Confederate States: A Memoir*, I, 530.

troversy over slavery which followed its passage, defeated all the attempts of President Pierce to secure national conciliation.

A prominent characteristic of the Pierce administration was the development of a vigorous foreign policy, manifested by the many treaties negotiated with foreign countries. Seldom has any administration pursued a more aggressive foreign policy than that exhibited in the first two years of Pierce's term of office. In his inaugural address, Pierce defined his position on expansion. He declared: ''The policy of my administration will not be controlled by any timid forebodings of evil from expansion. Indeed, it is not to be disguised that our attitude as a nation, and our position on the globe render the acquisition of certain possessions, not within our jurisdiction, eminently important for our protection.'' [20] This statement referred mainly to Cuba, and the acquisition of that island to the United States was the great desire of the administration. Although Pierce failed to secure Cuba, there took place during his term of office, the controversy with Spain over the Black Warrior affair, and the framing of the Ostend Manifesto. Contemporary with the negotiations with Mexico, there were also made a treaty of annexation with Hawaii; Perry's treaty with Japan; a reciprocity treaty with Canada, besides numerous less important agreements.[31] The dignity of the American nation was boldly championed abroad, as is seen in the abolition of the Danish Sound dues and the refusal to indemnify the British and French claimants for the damages resulting from the American destruction of Greytown. It is in connection with this background

[20] Richardson, J. D., *Messages and Papers of the Presidents*, V, 198.

[21] Moore, *Pol. Science Quar.* XXX, 377–396.

that the Gadsden treaty must be studied. It must be considered as one of the results of the vigorous foreign policy of the first year of the Pierce administration.

Almost contemporary with the change of administration in the United States, a revolution occurred in Mexico, and Santa Anna again came into power. On October 20, 1852, the Jalisco or Guadalajara Plan was signed at the city of Guadalajara, which declared for the recall of Santa Anna and for the federal constitution of 1824.[22] This plan was made the basis for the opposition to President Arista. Arista was forced to resign on January 6, 1853.[23] His successor, Ceballos, held office one month, in which time he dissolved Congress and adhered to the Plan of Jalisco.[24] General Lombardini was then invested with the executive power until an election for a president could be held.[25]

A great leader was needed to bring order out of the strife and to check the Indian raids in the northern states. In this state of affairs, the Mexicans again eagerly turned to their old hero, Santa Anna. His patriotism and services to Mexico were remembered and the soldiers were favorably inclined toward him.[26] There was little opposition to Santa Anna in the election which occurred in February and March, 1853.[27] By March 3, seventeen of the states had voted for Santa Anna, with only one opposed.[28] On March 17, he was declared elected and on April 20, he took the oath of office as President of Mexico.[29]

Once more there was a semblance of government in

[22] *Collección de las leyes fundamentales que han regido en la República Mexicana*, 300–303.

[23] See page 8.

[24] *Collección de la leyes fundamentales*, 307.

[25] *Ibid.*, 310.

[26] Bancroft, H. H., *History of Mexico*, V, 623–624.

[27] *Ibid.*

[28] Washington *Union*, Apr. 1, 1853.

[29] *Collección de las leyes fundamentales*, 317.

Mexico, but it was under the absolute control of one individual. On April 22, 1853, Santa Anna issued the "Bases" for the administration of government until a constitution could be promulgated.[30] No provision was made for an elective legislative body. Executive and legislative power was assumed by himself, with a council of twenty-one persons, of his own appointment as assistants. A union was at once made with the Church, through the appointment of a bishop as the head of the council.[31] Freedom of the press was denied by a decree of April 25, 1853.[32] Santa Anna's attitude toward America was shown by the dismissal from the army of all who voluntarily gave their parole to abstain from bearing arms against the United States in the Mexican War.[33] A decree was issued for the punishment of all treasonable acts committed by Mexicans in the war with the United States.[34] His absolute power culminated in a *pronunciamiento*, in which he proclaimed himself *"Serenissima Altesa,"* with dictatorial power.[35]

Doubtless the new administration in the United States would soon have taken steps to settle the disputes with Mexico, but critical conditions on the Mexican border opened the subject within the first month of the new regime. A dispute had arisen between the territory of New Mexico and the state of Chihuahua in regard to the jurisdiction over the Mesilla valley. Prior to the Bartlett-Condé compromise, the people in this valley had voted

[30] *El Siglo Diez y Nueve,* Apr. 24, 1853.

[31] Conkling to Marcy, May 2, 1853, Dept. of State, Des., Mex., vol. 17, no. 34.

[32] *El Monitor Republicano,* Apr. 30, 1853.

[33] Conkling to Marcy, May 4, 1853, Dept. of State, Des., Mex., vol. 17, no. 36.

[34] *Ibid.*

[35] Gadsden to Marcy, Sept. 17, 1853, *ibid.,* vol. 18, no. 5.

in New Mexico and had considered themselves American citizens.[36]   When the boundary difficulty arose, they had at once petitioned the governor of New Mexico to protect them from Mexico.[37]   In the meanwhile, the officials of the state of Chihuahua took possession of the disputed territory and extended Mexican authority over it.[38]   It was decreed by the Mexican officials that no one could hold land except Mexican citizens and thus the Americans were, without compensation, dispossessed of their property.[39]

This action on the part of Mexico caused great dissatisfaction on the southwestern border and especially in the territory of New Mexico.   Governor J. S. Calhoun was asked by the New Mexicans to retaliate, but ·he refused, because, as the New Mexican paper sarcastically wrote, ''it was not a part of his policy to protect the interests of his countrymen.'' [40]   Calhoun's successor, William C. Lane, took a different attitude, for, as he stated, he considered himself ''appointed Governor of all New Mexico, and not a part.'' [41]   As the federal government had taken no steps to regain the disputed region, Lane took it upon himself to preserve this region to the territory of New Mexico. In a proclamation of March 13, 1853, he stated that the Bartlett-Condé boundary line was not valid, that the disputed territory belonged to New Mexico, and that Chihuahua had failed to protect this territory.[42]   Upon his own responsibility, and in behalf of the United States, he retook possession of this disputed region, this possession to be

[36] Santa Fé *Weekly Gazette*, July 23, 1853.

[37] *S. Ex. Docs.* (665), 32 Cong., 2 sess., VII, no. 41, p. 13.

[38] Santa Fé *Weekly Gazette*, May 7, 1853.

[39] Meriwether to Marcy, Aug. 31, 1853, Dept. of State, Misc. Let.

[40] Santa Fé *Weekly Gazette*, May 7, 1853.

[41] Lane to Conkling, May 13, 1853, Dept. of State, Misc. Let.

[42] Copy of proclamation, Dept. of State, Misc. Let., Mar.–Apr. 1853.

provisional on the part of the United States until the
boundary dispute was settled. Governor Trias of Chihuahua replied with a counter-proclamation, in which he
declared that he would preserve the national honor against
all aggressions.[43]

The inhabitants of the southwest were anxious to re-
claim the disputed territory by force of arms. Lane
called upon Colonel Sumner for the aid of the federal
military forces for this purpose, but the latter refused to
comply with the request.[44] With the inhabitants of New
Mexico it was different. At a meeting of the citizens of
Santa Fé, of which congressional delegate, Hugh N. Smith,
was chairman, the action of Governor Lane was praised,
and he was promised the earnest support of the people.[45]
The General Assembly of California was in session when
the news of the Lane-Trias affair came. On June 2, a
resolution was offered in the assembly, the preamble of
which stated that as war might be expected, a committee
of three should draft a joint resolution which would
authorize certain persons to organize ten companies of
men and go to the Mesilla valley at their own cost, until in
case of war requisition should be made on the state for
troops.[46] After a lengthy debate, the resolution was laid
on the table, but the correspondent adds that ''the course
of Governor Trias is on all hands spoken of as outrageous,
nobody doubting that Governor Lane was in the right.''
Volunteers from both New Mexico and Texas offered to
help Governor Lane recapture the country by force.[47]

The Lane-Trias affair caused much excitement in Mex-

[43] Santa Fé *Weekly Gazette*, May 14, 1853.
[44] Lane to Marcy, Mar. 24, 1853, Dept. of State, Misc. Let.
[45] Santa Fé *Weekly Gazette*, May 14, 1853.
[46] Washington *Union*, June 12, 1853.
[47] Lane to Marcy, Mar. 24, 1853, Dept. of State, Misc. Let.

ico. Santa Anna ordered Governor Trias to march his troops into the disputed territory and resist all attempts of the Americans to take possession of the same.[48] Trias, with a thousand men, marched to the border of the disputed region.[49] The Mexican press was bitter in the denunciation of Lane's action. *El Eco Del Comercio* of Vera Cruz considered it a flagrant and criminal transgression of the laws of society.[50] It favored the destruction of Mexico in an unequal combat with America rather than the endurance of such insults. A solemn protest against the action of Lane was made to Conkling by the Mexican government.[51] Conkling disavowed Lane's move as the policy of the United States. In a communication to Lane, he severely criticized him for his illegal step.[52]

The matter was settled, however, without resort to arms. Lane did not take possession of the Mesilla valley, as he had accomplished his intention of forcing the federal government to take action.[53] Secretary Marcy justified Lane's action, in his claim to the disputed region, but any proceedings to hold it by force were not approved.[54] Conkling was severely criticized for his dispatches of reproval to Lane.[55] Lane was soon recalled and David Meriwether, of Kentucky, was appointed governor of the territory of New Mexico. He was instructed not to take forcible possession of the valley, and to avoid collision with

[48] Doyle to Clarendon, July 3, 1853, F. O., Mex., vol. 260, no. 71.
[49] Hendree to Marcy, Apr. 23, 1853, Dept. of State, Misc. Let.
[50] From N. O. *Daily Picayune*, July 2, 1853.
[51] Conkling to Marcy, Apr. 8, 1853, Dept. of State, Des., Mex., vol. 17, no. 31.
[52] Conkling to Lane, Apr. 8, 1853, Dept. of State, Misc. Let.
[53] Santa Fé *Weekly Gazette*, May 7, 1853.
[54] Marcy to Conkling, May 18, 1853, Dept. of State, Inst., Mex., vol. 16, no. 20.
[55] *Ibid.*

Mexico, as such actions would embarrass the adjustment of the difficulty.[56]

The Lane-Trias affair had thus precipitated the Mexican situation. In order to avoid conflict on the frontier and to adjust all the issues with Mexico, the administration decided to make a new treaty with that nation. In the change of ministers to foreign countries, Conkling was recalled from Mexico, and James Gadsden, of Charleston, South Carolina, was chosen as the American representative to settle the difficulties between the two countries.

James Gadsden was a member of the famous Gadsden family of Charleston, South Carolina; a grandson of Christopher Gadsden of Revolutionary War fame.[57] After his graduation from Yale College, in 1806, he returned to Charleston and became a merchant.[58] At the outbreak of War of 1812, he enlisted in the army as Second Lieutenant in the Engineer Corps, and saw active service on the Canadian border.[59] After the close of the war, he was detailed as an expert engineer to accompany General Andrew Jackson on an expedition to inspect the fortifications of the Gulf of Mexico and the southwestern frontier. Immediately a great friendship was formed between the two soldiers, and Jackson made Gadsden his confidential aide-de-camp.[60] He served with Jackson in the Florida campaign of 1817–18 and it was through his efforts that the papers were captured which led to the execution of Arbuthnot and Ambrister.[61] A fort which Jackson built

[56] Marcy to Meriwether, May 28, 1853, Dept. of State, Dom. Let., vol. 41.

[57] Dexter, F. B., *Yale Graduates*, VI, 28.

[58] *Ibid.*, 29.

[59] *Ibid.*

[60] *Ibid.*

[61] Jackson to Calhoun, Apr. 20, 1818, *Amer. State Papers, Mil. Aff.*, I, 701.

in Florida was named Fort Gadsden as a tribute to the activity of Gadsden in this campaign.[62]

Greater friendship is seldom to be found between public characters than that which existed between Jackson and Gadsden, as for example in 1819 Gadsden informed Jackson that he would retire from the army and move to Tennessee, for "near you I would wish to end my days." [63] Together they formed a company for land speculation in Tennessee.[64] Gadsden was Jackson's main helper in his fight in Congress over the Florida campaign, and he made several trips to Washington in the interest of Jackson. He was a strong supporter of Jackson in the presidential campaign of 1824 at which time he published a campaign biography of the general.[65] In 1831, Jackson appointed Gadsden to a position in the War Department at Washington, because, as he informed Gadsden, "it will bring you near me." [66]

This friendship with Jackson was of great advantage to Gadsden in his military career, for through Jackson's influence he was rapidly advanced. In 1818 he was made captain, and in 1820, at Jackson's suggestion, he was appointed Inspector General of the Southern District, with the rank of colonel.[67] In 1821, again through Jackson's influence, Gadsden was appointed Adjutant General of the army by President Monroe.[68] Professional jealousy and political reasons caused the rejection of his nomination in the Senate by a vote of 20 to 23.[69] Gadsden ex-

[62] *Ibid.* to *ibid.*, Mar. 25, 1818, *ibid.*, 698.

[63] Gadsden to Jackson, Feb. 18, 1819, Jackson Papers, vol. 52.

[64] *Ibid.* to *ibid.*, Sept. 28, 1818, *ibid.*, vol. 50.

[65] Dexter, *Yale Graduates*, VI, 29.

[66] Jackson to Gadsden, July 21, 1831, Jackson Papers, vol. 78.

[67] Calhoun to Monroe, Aug. 29, 1818, *Calhoun Correspondence,* Amer. His. Assoc., *Annual Report*, 1899, II, 139.

[68] Jackson to Monroe, Jan. 21, 1823, Monroe Papers.

[69] *S. Ex. Journal*, III, 280.

plained the rejection as due to his friendship for Jackson and Calhoun.[70]  Gadsden never forgot the action of the Senate, and all through his life he was a bitter enemy of that body, and of Van Buren and Benton, who voted for the rejection of his nomination.

Gadsden retired from the army but President Monroe at once appointed him commissioner to treat with the Seminole Indians in Florida for the sale of their lands and for their removal to reservations.[71]  In September, 1823, Gadsden negotiated the treaty of Fort Moultrie with the Seminoles.  This treaty opened the northern part of Florida for colonization.[72]  After this task was completed Gadsden was appointed by President Monroe to survey the Indian reservations and to build the first government roads in Florida.[73]  The fertile land in Florida attracted the attention of Gadsden, and in 1825 he disposed of his property in Tennessee and settled in Florida.[74]  In 1824, President Monroe appointed him a member of the first Legislative Council of the territory of Florida.[75]

Gadsden soon found farming in Florida very distasteful. He informed Jackson that his active public career had unfitted him for the dull life of a Florida planter.  He yearned for the pursuit of a profession more congenial to his habits and taste than that of ''plowing the soil and subduing the forest.''[76]  The joy of country life, he

[70] Gadsden to Jackson, Apr. 10, 1822; July 24, 1836, Jackson Papers, vols. 62, 95.

[71] Calhoun to Gadsden, Apr. 7, 1823, *Amer. State Papers, Ind. Aff.*, II, 431.

[72] Copy of treaty, *ibid.*, 429–430.

[73] Calhoun to Gadsden, Nov. 4, 1823, *ibid.*, II, 441.

[74] Gadsden to Jackson, July 8, 1824, Jackson Papers, vol. 65.

[75] *S. Ex. Journal*, III, 365.

[76] Gadsden to Jackson, June 24, 1833, Jackson Papers, vol. 84.

thought, was only to be found in the imagination of the poets.[77]

Accordingly, he turned to politics, and from 1825 to 1838 he was almost annually a candidate for some office in the territory of Florida. He made many hard campaigns for the position of territorial delegate to Congress, but was always defeated by his rival, J. M. White. The closest race was in 1831, when he was defeated by only eighty votes out of a total of four thousand.[78] In this campaign, Gadsden ran on a nullification platform. The publication in March, 1831, of a circular in which he championed the nullification theory of his native state,[79] caused a break in his friendship with President Jackson which lasted for several years.

Gadsden's defeats for political offices, his distaste for agriculture, and the Seminole War in Florida, 1835–1844, caused him to leave Florida, and in 1839 he returned to his native city. Here he entered into mercantile business. In 1840 he was elected President of the Louisville, Charleston, and Cincinnati Railroad.[80] This position he held for ten years.

This railroad was the result of the dream of R. Y. Hayne to connect Charleston with Cincinnati and thus to draw the trade of the West to Charleston.[81] Gadsden also had been interested in such a project, and had been selected by the state of South Carolina in 1835 to act as chief engineer for the survey of the proposed route.[82] In order to build

[77] Ibid. to ibid., June 11, 1831, ibid., vol. 78.

[78] Tallahassee, The Floridian and Advocate, June 21, 1831.

[79] Ibid., Apr. 7, 1831.

[80] Charleston Daily Courier, Mar. 19, 1840.

[81] For a detailed account of this project, see Jervey, T. D., Robert Y. Hayne and His Times, and Phillips, U. B., A History of Transportation in the Eastern Cotton Belt to 1860.

[82] The Floridian, July 30, 1836.

this railroad, a company was formed, with a capital of $4,000,000, of which sum South Carolina, North Carolina, Tennessee, and Kentucky were each to subscribe a certain amount.[83]  The one hundred and thirty-six miles of track of the South Carolina Canal and Railroad Company, between Charleston and Hamburg, South Carolina, were purchased as the nucleus of the road.[84]  No additional track was laid, as the panic of 1837 and dissensions within the company halted all progress.  A dispute arose within the company between John C. Calhoun and Gadsden on one side and Hayne on the other as to the most practicable route for the railroad.  In the meantime the other states withdrew from the company, so that in 1840, when the Calhoun group came into the control of affairs and Gadsden was elected President, the company was burdened with a debt of $3,000,000, and had only one hundred and thirty-six miles of track to offset this deficit.[85]  The high-sounding title of the railroad was dropped.  After 1840 it was known simply as the South Carolina Railroad.

Gadsden used his position as President of the South Carolina Railroad to further his plan of a southern railroad to the Pacific Ocean.  His interest in railroads went further than the South Carolina Railroad.  His sole aim in connection with this road was, as he declared, to bring South Carolina into more intimate relations with the West.[86]  His plan of a transcontinental railroad, with Charleston as the eastern terminus, Gadsden wrote in 1845 had "been conceived many years ago," [87] but it was after 1845 that his greatest zeal for such a route was manifested. By means of the press, by correspondence, and through

[83] Phillips, *History of Transportation*, 186.
[84] Charleston *Daily Courier*, Oct. 21, 1840.
[85] *Ibid.*, Feb. 5, 1851.
[86] *Ibid.*, Feb. 8, 1851.
[87] Gadsden to Shanks, Sept. 17, 1845, Gadsden Papers.

conventions, he kept this plan before the public.  He was
one of the prime movers of the Memphis Commercial Convention of 1845, where as chairman of the Committee on
Railroads he urged the construction of a railroad to the
Pacific and recommended it to the South as an advantageous investment.[88]  He designated the route along the
Gila River as the shortest and most practicable for the
southern road.  After the Memphis convention his efforts
were directed toward the connection of all railroads in the
various southern states, so as to have one continuous line
from Charleston to the Mississippi River.[89]  He informed
A. J. Donelson in 1846 that, upon his return from Ger-
many, he would be able to ride on a railroad from Charleston to Nashville.[90]

Gadsden's plan for the construction of more miles of
railroad did not appeal to the stockholders, who were de-
manding dividends, and in 1850 he was removed from the
presidency of the company.[91]  "The reputation of having
originated the Grand and Western Extension," one stock-
holder declared, afforded little consolation to the sufferers
who desired profits.[92]  But Gadsden was still the cham-
pion of the southern route in 1853, when he was appointed
minister to Mexico.

Gadsden was a typical southerner of the *ante bellum*
days.  In 1820 he had declared to Jackson that no parties
were more to be deprecated than those which were based
upon sectional interests.[93]  By 1835 however he had com-
pletely changed, for he asserted that if the South thought

[88] *De Bow's Commercial Review*, Jan. 1846 (I, 27–33).

[89] Gadsden to a friend, July 16, 1854, in N. Y. *Journal of Commerce*, Aug. 17, 1854.

[90] Gadsden to Donelson, Mar. 30, 1846, Donelson Papers, vol. 11.

[91] Charleston *Daily Courier*, Feb. 15, 1850.

[92] *Ibid.*, Jan. 22, 1849.

[93] Gadsden to Jackson, Dec. 8, 1820, Jackson Papers, vol. 58.

it necessary to stand for the preservation of its rights and liberties, he "would not be the last to do his duty." [94] He was an ardent exponent of the theory of nullification. By 1844 the policy of Calhoun was too slow for Gadsden,[95] and in 1850 he was one of the leaders of the secession movement in South Carolina.[96] Slavery, he thought, was a social blessing, and the abolitionism of the North he considered the greatest curse of the nation.[97] Consequently, he favored the extension of slavery. In 1851, he was a leader of a group of southern planters who memorialized the Assembly of California, for permission to form a colony in the southern part of that state. To a friend he declared that these planters would lead from five hundred to eight hundred slaves to California.[98] He was anxious to unite the South and West, so that the anti-slavery and anti-Southern program of the North might be held in check. The Memphis Convention of 1845 was favored by Gadsden as a means to enlist the western states "as allies of the Great Commercial and Agricultural interests . . . instead of the Tax-Gathering and Monopolistic interests of the North." [99] Gadsden was a firm advocate of free trade. In 1844 he declared that if he were a Texan, he would hesitate between the offer of annexation to the United States, and independence under a free trade system.[100] These views, with his ardent championship of a southern railroad to the Pacific, he carried to Mexico, and his mission there was marked by the attempt to put them

[94] Gadsden to Murat, Oct. 18, 1835, in *The Floridian*, Nov. 7, 1835.

[95] Gadsden to Jackson, Aug. 1, 1844, Jackson Papers, vol. 112.

[96] Hamer, P. M., *The Secession Movement in South Carolina, 1847–1852*, 35.

[97] Gadsden to Murat, Oct. 18, 1835, in *The Floridian*, Nov. 7, 1835.

[98] Gadsden to Estes, Dec. 10, 1851, in Charleston *Daily Courier*, Feb. 7, 1852.

[99] Gadsden to Calhoun, Oct. 9, 1845, *Calhoun Correspondence*, 1062.

[100] Gadsden to Jackson, Aug. 1, 1844, Jackson Papers, vol. 112.

into practice in connection with the relations between the United States and Mexico.

During the Mexican War, Gadsden, like Calhoun, was opposed to any large acquisition of Mexican territory by the United States. He declared to Calhoun, January 23, 1848, that "the great object at this time is to arrest the mad designs of conquest. . . . The cry of the administration on that subject has been echoed and the whole pack of hungry land hounds have opened upon the scent."[101] It was his hope that the Whigs and the sober-minded patriots of the Democratic party would combine against large acquisition and would rescue the country from "the catastrophe into which the Presidential making and a blind ambition of conquest is hurrying Polk and his advisers." Gadsden desired only a natural boundary between the two countries. The Sierra Madre range, he thought, was the natural boundary that should be placed between the Anglo-Saxon and the Spanish races.[102] He held this same view when he went as minister to Mexico. He desired no acquisition of Mexican territory simply for American expansion. To secure a natural boundary between the two countries was the basis for his attempts to purchase a large amount of Mexican territory.

As in other diplomatic appointments, the influence of Jefferson Davis is seen in the selection of Gadsden as minister to Mexico. Davis informed Gadsden of his appointment before Secretary Marcy sent an official communication to that effect.[103] The New York *Herald* asserted that Davis was responsible for the appointment, as it later declared that "not the least interesting portion of the

[101] Calhoun Papers, from Boucher, C. S., ''In Re that Aggressive Slavocracy,'' in *Miss. Val. His. Rev.*, VIII, 37.

[102] *Ibid.*

[103] Gadsden to Marcy, May 23, 1853, Dept. of State, Des., Mex., vol. 18.

treaty is the manner in which Jefferson Davis managed to get General Gadsden appointed without the aid of a single voice from his state.''[104]   The appointment was apparently a surprise to Gadsden, for he wrote to a commercial house of Washington that the appointment took him by surprise, ''but as a voluntary offering from the President it is the higher appreciated.''[105]

The Charleston *Daily Courier* praised the appointment of Gadsden,[106] which, however, was severely criticized by ex-Governor Hammond of South Carolina.[107]   Gadsden's appointment was attributed by Hammond to the fact that he was a Gadsden and a pet of Jackson.   Hammond could not understand why Gadsden desired to go to Mexico or anywhere, as he could but add one more failure to his list of failures, which ''embraced every undertaking of his useless life.'' ''Gadsden,'' he declared, ''has been bolstered up from all quarters and put forward and yet never does anything.''[108]

Gadsden gladly accepted the appointment and at once began to gather information for his mission.   He inquired for the latest statistics on Mexican trade, for he thought that better commercial relations between the two countries would accomplish more than diplomacy.[109]   With this opportunity to settle the boundary line dispute, he was determined to secure a line that would guarantee the gratification of his pet desire, a southern railroad route. Before he received his instructions, Gadsden urged Secretary Marcy to send A. B. Gray as his agent to the disputed

[104] N. Y. *Herald*, Apr. 7, 1854.
[105] Washington *Union*, May 24, 1853.
[106] Charleston *Daily Courier*, May 17, 1853.
[107] Hammond to Simms, May 17, 1853, Hammond Papers, vol. 19.
[108] *Ibid.*
[109] Washington *Union*, May 24, 1853.

region.[110]   He desired a detailed knowledge of the country, so as to preclude the necessity of a future revision of the boundary line.[111]   Gray was very much interested in the suggestion and assured Marcy that the expense of such an investigation would not exceed several thousand dollars.[112] In a lengthy document he explained to Marcy how he would investigate the region of the Rio Grande and Gila rivers and the Gulf of California, ascertain the best limits for a right of way, and then report to Gadsden in Mexico City.[113]   The proposals of Gadsden and Gray were rejected by Secretary Marcy.   Gray, however, went to the Mexican border in September, 1853, as the engineer of a railroad company of New York.   At that late date he again offered to collect the information that was desired by Gadsden, and without any cost to the Department of State.[114]   Information was furnished Marcy by Gray, but it came too late to aid in the negotiation of a treaty with Mexico.[115]

The attitude of the new administration toward the Mexican situation is shown in the lengthy instructions to Gadsden of July 15, 1853.[116]   It was admitted by Secretary Marcy that the last war had embittered the Mexicans toward America.   Gadsden was urged to emphasize the friendship of the American government with the Mexican people and to inspire in them a reciprocal feeling toward the United States.

In regard to the Garay grant, Gadsden was instructed

[110] Gadsden to Marcy, July 7, 1853, Marcy Papers, vol. 40.

[111] *Ibid.* to *ibid.*, July 19, 1853, Dept. of State, Des., Mex., vol. 18.

[112] Gray to Marcy, Aug. 12, 1853, Marcy Papers, vol. 41.

[113] *Ibid.* to *ibid.*, no date, *ibid.*, vol. 46.

[114] *Ibid.* to *ibid.*, Sept. 12, 1853, *ibid.*, vol. 42.

[115] *Ibid.* to *ibid.*, Apr. 15, 1854, Dept. of State, Misc. Let.

[116] Marcy to Gadsden, July 15, 1853, Dept. of State, Inst., Mex., vol. 16, no. 3.

not to resume negotiations at that time, and no encourage-
ment was to be given the Mexican government that the
Conkling convention would be approved by the United
States. That convention was declared to be in direct conflict with the Garay grant. If it were accepted, Marcy
continued, it would imply an abandonment of any further
attempt to induce Mexico to respect the rights of the
assignees under the Garay contract. Further instructions
on this subject were promised at some future time.

The view held by the former administration in reference
to the boundary dispute was not accepted by President
Pierce. The Bartlett-Condé line was declared to be null,
as article V of the treaty of Guadalupe Hidalgo stipulated
that both the commissioner and the surveyor must agree
upon the line. Gadsden was to urge upon Mexico, as
the view of the government, that the line had never been
legally established, and he was to obtain the consent of the
Mexican government to have it run and marked. The intention of Governor Lane to possess the disputed territory
by force was not sanctioned. Gadsden was instructed to
insist that while the boundary remained unadjusted,
neither country should take possession of the Mesilla valley.

In reference to the transcontinental railroad, Marcy
pointed out that better knowledge of the country had dem-
onstrated the great difficulty and even the impossibility
of the construction of a railroad along the Gila River,
within the space mentioned by the treaty of Guadalupe
Hidalgo. An ideal route was to be found, however, at a
greater distance from the river on the Mexican side. As
Mexico would benefit from such a road, Marcy thought
that it should agree to change the boundary so as to give
sufficient territory to the United States for a practicable
railroad route. If Mexico would accept such a proposal,
Gadsden was promised information in regard to the coun-

try south of the Gila River. An eligible route for a railroad was declared to be the sole object of the desire of the American government for a change in the boundary line. Marcy was not in a position to state the amount of money to be paid for such a cession but he thought that it should be acquired for a moderate sum.

If Mexico agreed to treat for a new boundary line, Gadsden was instructed not to press the American claim to the disputed territory, but to merge it in the negotiation for the former. In such a negotiation, the claims of the citizens of the United States against Mexico and "the pretended claims of Mexican citizens under article XI" were to be included. The interpretation of article XI by the administration was that the United States was bound only to restrain the Indian incursions into Mexico in the same manner as if they were directed against American citizens. This would include no financial indemnity for the sufferers. The failure to enforce this article was attributed to the neglect of the Mexican government to protect its citizens. Although the validity of the claims of Mexico under that article was denied, the administration was willing to negotiate on that topic in the final disposition of all matters. Gadsden's mission therefore, was to secure a new line which would give the United States additional territory for a practicable railroad route, a release from the obligations of article XI, and a settlement of all claims between the two governments. For such an adjustment, Marcy declared that the United States would pay a liberal sum. An adjustment of the commercial relations between the two countries was a task also assigned to Gadsden.

Steps toward a settlement of the diplomatic issues were taken as soon as Gadsden reached Mexico City. Gadsden arrived at Vera Cruz on August 4, 1853, and on August 17, he had his first conference with Santa Anna.[117] Correspondence concerning the differences between the two countries was begun on August 20, by Bonilla, Mexican Minister of Foreign Relations.[118] In this dispatch he complained of the filibustering expeditions of American citizens into the state of Sonora. On August 30, Bonilla, addressed a lengthy communication to Gadsden which dealt with the Indian depredations in the northern states.[119] He demanded that the stipulations of article XI be made effective by the adoption of measures for the redress of these injuries and for the punishment of the Indians. Gadsden was asked to communicate the contents of the note to his government.

Gadsden replied to this communication on September 9.[120] He denied that the United States was bound by the treaty of Guadalupe Hidalgo to indemnify Mexico for the damages which had been inflicted by the Indians. He pointed out that two former treaties of the United States, one with Spain in 1795 and the other with Mexico in 1831, had contained similar provisions to that of article XI, and that although Indian raids had then involved the loss of property and life, no demand for indemnity was ever preferred by either party. In the final paragraphs of the note, Gadsden outlined the differences between the two countries, and informed Bonilla that he was ready to entertain propositions for the adjustment of the same.

Bonilla refused to answer Gadsden's note of September 9, but it led to a conference between Gadsden and Santa Anna on September 25.[121] The result of this interview was an understanding between them that the disputed

117 Gadsden to Marcy, Aug. 17, 1853, Dept. of State, Des., Mex., vol. 18, no. 1.

118 Bonilla to Gadsden, Aug. 20, 1853, *ibid.*, vol. 18, with no. 2.

119 *Ibid.* to *ibid.*, Aug. 30, 1853, *ibid.*, vol. 18, with no. 4.

120 Gadsden to Bonilla, Sept. 9, 1853, *ibid.*

121 Gadsden to Marcy, Oct. 3, 1853, *ibid.*, vol. 18, no. 7.

territory should remain in *statu quo*. Santa Anna also agreed to negotiate with Gadsden for a new boundary which would involve the sale of Mexican territory, so as to reconcile the conflicting interpretations of articles V, VI, and XI of the treaty of Guadalupe Hidalgo.

On October 2, another conference was held in which Gadsden suggested the sale of a large tract of Mexican territory, so as to procure a mountain or desert boundary between the two nations.[122] He pointed out to Santa Anna that "no power in the world could prevent the whole valley of the Rio Grande from being under the same Government . . . either western Texas must come back to the Mexican Government or the states of Tamaulipas, New Leon, Coahuila and Chihuahua would by successive revolutions become united with Texas." This proposal was not in harmony with his instructions but it was in harmony with the view Gadsden had expressed in 1848 that a natural boundary was necessary for peaceful relations between the two countries. Santa Anna would not listen to such a proposal, because he declared that his nation would be strongly opposed to any other dismemberment of the territory than was necessary to settle the boundary dispute. He would enter into no negotiations other than those which contemplated the settlement of the existing disagreements. The conference ended with the declaration of Santa Anna that he would welcome proposals for such an adjustment.

Further negotiations were delayed by Gadsden's lack of instructions. Santa Anna desired to settle all the issues between the two countries in one treaty, but Gadsden had no definite instructions on the subjects of private claims and the isthmian grants.[123] In the meantime, Gadsden's

[122] *Ibid.* to *ibid.*, Oct. 3, 1853, *ibid.*, vol. 18, no. 6.
[123] *Ibid.* to *ibid.*, Oct. 17; Nov. 3, 1853, *ibid.*, vol. 18, nos. 10, 12.

policy was to go slowly and to force Mexico to offer proposals. To show any anxiety in the matter, he declared,
would cause Mexico to think that the United States would
pay any sum for a settlement of the difficulties. He also
used this opportunity to send an agent to El Paso to obtain information on the country near the boundary line.[124]

The Mexican diplomatic policy was to stress the Indian
depredations. Exaggerated accounts of destruction by
the Indians were circulated daily, so that they might
reach the American minister's office.[125] Santa Anna
ordered the collection of all the Indian claims of the frontier states.[126] These claims were constantly placed before
Gadsden, and Almonte was ordered to press these claims
at Washington, which he did in a note to Secretary Marcy
on October 22, 1853.[127] He suggested that these claims
should be adjudicated before a mixed tribunal. Marcy,
however, refused to discuss the subject with Almonte, and
informed him that Gadsden had been instructed to settle
that matter in Mexico City.[128] The belief, prevalent in
Mexico that the United States would pay any price for a
railroad route, also made the Mexican attitude more
arrogant.

Although Santa Anna had been elected by an over-
whelming majority in March, 1853, his policy of central-
ization of the government immediately aroused opposition
in the Mexican states.[129] Santa Anna, when he became
President, found the treasury empty, the American in-

[124] Ibid. to ibid., Oct. 3, 1853, ibid., vol. 18, no. 6.

[125] Ibid. to ibid., Aug. 31, 1853, ibid., vol. 18, no. 2.

[126] Ibid. to ibid., Oct. 3, 1853, ibid., vol. 18, no. 7.

[127] Almonte to Marcy, Oct. 22, 1853, Dept. of State, Notes to
Dept., Mex. Leg., vol. 7.

[128] Marcy to Almonte, Dec. 22, 1853, Dept. of State, Notes from
Dept., Mex. Leg., vol. 6.

[129] For a more detailed account of the administration of Santa
Anna, see Bancroft, *Mexico*, V, 615–645.

demnity squandered, and a tremendous debt upon his hands. The heavy taxation and forced loans which were levied in order to rehabilitate the treasury, injured the trade and industry of the nation. Debts remained unpaid, the frontiers were neglected, and ruinous contracts were conceded to favorites, all of which added to the discontent of the people and aroused resentment against Santa Anna. Already, in the summer of 1853, several revolts had occurred, which, however had been suppressed by Santa Anna.

These internal conditions of Mexico were pictured in the lengthy official and private dispatches of Gadsden to the Department of State. The tenor of all his notes was that Santa Anna was in great need of money, which fact would influence any negotiation. On August 17, Marcy was informed that the amount to be paid, and not the amount of territory to be ceded, was the consideration with Mexico.[130] A few weeks later Gadsden reported that the deficit of $17,000,000 in the Mexican treasury would force Santa Anna to turn to the United States for financial relief.[131] He asked Marcy for a sum of $10,000,000 in order to be in a position to treat with Santa Anna whenever the latter was in dire straits for money. On October 3, Gadsden believed that he could conclude a treaty which would reconcile all the differences, but, as he informed Marcy, "they must be paid for."[132] In a private letter to Marcy on October 18, Gadsden wrote, "This is a Government of plunder and necessity; we can rely on no other influence but an appeal to both."[133]

Gadsden not only stressed Santa Anna's financial neces-

---

[130] Gadsden to Marcy, Aug. 17, 1853, Dept. of State, Des., Mex., vol. 18, no. 1.

[131] *Ibid. to ibid.*, Sept. 5, 1853, *ibid.*, vol. 18, private.

[132] *Ibid. to ibid.*, Oct. 3, 1853, *ibid.*

[133] *Ibid. to ibid.*, Oct. 18, 1853, *ibid.*

sities but he also pointed out that his government might soon be overthrown. Marcy was informed on September 5, that certain forces were at work which aimed to dismiss Santa Anna's dynasty.[134] On September 18, Gadsden was of the opinion that he would soon have to treat with a new party.[135] By October 3, he was certain that a revolution was brewing in Mexico.[136] These dispatches were confirmed by the reports in American newspapers of the expected fall of Santa Anna in the near future.

These reports of Gadsden led the American administration to take action. It was feared that a golden opportunity for the negotiation of a favorable treaty with Mexico might be lost through delay. Accordingly, on October 22, 1853, Christopher L. Ward, of Bradford county, Pennsylvania was sent as a special secret messenger to Mexico, to communicate verbal instructions to Gadsden for the negotiation of a treaty.[137]

Ward was sent to Mexico, as Secretary Marcy later explained to Gadsden, because "it was thought that there was at the time he was sent a very critical state of things in regard to the ruling power in that country, and that immediate pecuniary means would be indispensable for its maintenance: and to provide these means in the apprehended emergency a liberal concession of territory might be readily made. But at the same time it was suggested that should it in any way become publicly known that such cession was contemplated, that fact would not only defeat

---

[134] *Ibid.* to *ibid.*, Sept. 5, 1853, *ibid.*

[135] *Ibid.* to *ibid.*, Sept. 18, 1853, *ibid.*

[136] *Ibid.* to *ibid.*, Oct. 3, 1853, *ibid.*

[137] Memorandum of Instructions to C. L. Ward, Oct. 22, 1853, Dept. of State, Special Missions, No. 3.

the object but overturn the existing government. It was, therefore, deemed imprudent to intrust written dispatches even in the hands of a special messenger. It was also apprehended at that time that the very unlimited power of Santa Anna might soon be circumscribed and he would not at a future period be able to do what his necessities would incline him to do in order to get the means to strengthen his doubtful rule."[138]

No written instructions were taken by Ward to Mexico, but in the archives of the Department of State at Washington, is filed a "Memorandum of Instructions" which Ward was to memorize and to communicate verbally to Gadsden.[139] According to this memorandum, Ward was to submit to Gadsden six possible boundary lines between the United States and Mexico, and the sum to be paid for each. The sum mentioned for each change of boundary was to include all the Mexican claims, both public and private, against the United States, except those under article XI of the treaty of Guadalupe Hidalgo. In addition to this, Gadsden was given the authority to include a reciprocal agreement for the release of Mexico from all American claims which had arisen under the treaty of Guadalupe Hidalgo.

For line No. 1, as designated on the accompanying map, Gadsden was authorized to pay any sum up to $50,000,000. This purchase would have included a large portion of what was then the northern part of the states of Coahuila, Chihuahua, Sonora, and all of Lower California. This line was preferred by President Pierce, who considered it "the best for both parties, because it would be a permanent

138 Marcy to Gadsden, Jan. 6, 1854, Dept. of State, Inst., Mex., vol. 16, no. 20.
139 Memorandum of Instructions to C. L. Ward, Oct. 22, 1853, Dept. of State, Special Missions, no. 3.

boundary, guarded and defended at much less expense than any other, thus removing all serious apprehensions of border difficulty.'' Even with this boundary, Gadsden was urged to get a stipulation for the release of the United States from the obligations of article XI. In the case of the other lines, however, it was considered still more important that there should be such a release.

Line No. 2, as traced by President Pierce and shown on the map, did not extend quite so far south as line No. 1, nor did it include Lower California. This territory was estimated to contain fifty thousand square miles, and Gadsden was instructed to offer $35,000,000 for it.

Line No. 3, which was traced still farther north in Mexico, included the Peninsula of Lower California. President Pierce estimated this region to contain sixty-eight thousand square miles, for which the sum of $30,000,000 was to be offered.

Line No. 4 was the same as line No. 3, with the exclusion of Lower California. It contained about eighteen thousand square miles. For this territory Gadsden was instructed to offer any sum up to $20,000,000.

Gadsden was informed that if it were impossible to secure any of the foregoing boundaries, then the object of a negotiation would be to get an eligible railroad route from the Rio Grande to California. A line along the parallel of 31° 48′ north latitude to the Gulf of California was considered a good boundary, as it gave the United States, perhaps, the best route for a railroad. For a release of all claims of damages under the treaty of Guadalupe Hidalgo, the abrogation of article XI, and a boundary line from Frontera or on the thirty-second parallel of north latitude, Gadsden was authorized to pay any sum up to $15,000,000. A port on the Gulf of California was desired by the administration, and Gadsden was instructed to keep

[Explanation of Map No. 2 on reverse]

EXPLANATION OF MAP NO. 2

Line No. 1.   Boundary line most desired by President Pierce.
Line No. 2.   Second boundary line desired by President Pierce.
Line No. 3.   Third boundary line designated by President Pierce.
Line No. 4.   Fourth boundary line designated by President Pierce.
Line No. 5.   Boundary line designated by President Pierce as sufficient to secure a southern railway route.
Line No. 6.   Boundary line designated by President Pierce as sufficient to secure a southern railway route.
Line No. 7.   Boundary line secured by Gadsden.
Line No. 8.   Boundary line designated by the Senate in the amended treaty which was defeated by the Senate.
Line No. 9.   Final boundary line between the two countries.
Line common to lines Nos. 1, 2, 3, 4.

Southeastern boundary line as agreed upon by Condé and Bartlett.
Southeastern boundary line as designated by Disturnell's map, and demanded by Surveyor Gray.

that fact in mind, in the negotiation for a new boundary line.

No mention was made in the memorandum of the Garay and Sloo grants and this fact is important in view of the actions of Ward when he reached Mexico City. The memorandum stated: "It is believed that the condition of things in Mexico will not admit of a protracted negotiation, and it has not been deemed expedient to complicate it with any other matter than a change of boundary and the reciprocal claims which have arisen under the present Treaty of Peace and Limits."

These instructions by their own terms looked toward the removal of all future border troubles, through the acquisition of a natural boundary between the two nations, the securing of territory for a railroad route, and the obtaining of a port on the Gulf of California. This purpose is further shown by the reports and recommendations of government officials. General Persifor F. Smith, military commander on the Mexican border, advised the administration to procure a mountain range for a boundary, in place of the open border along the Rio Grande.[140] The reduction of military expenses, in the defense of a border with only a few passes, would soon, he thought, pay all the cost of such a purchase of Mexican territory. Secretary Davis informed Congress in 1853, that since the Colorado River was not navigable, it was necessary for him, in the transportation of war supplies to the Mexican border to tranship on small boats or to haul the stores across the Mexican territory.[141] He pointed out the value to the United States of a port on the Gulf of California and declared that its necessity from a military standpoint required or justified no explanation. The first four boundary lines desig-

---

[140] Smith to Davis, Dec. 22, 1853, Davis Papers.
[141] *S. Ex. Docs.* (691), 33 Cong., 1 sess., II, no. 1, p. 25.

nated by President Pierce, and especially line No. 1, coincided with natural boundaries.[142]

A short sketch of the life of C. L. Ward is necessary for an understanding of what now took place in Mexico City. He was a native of Pennsylvania and from 1835 to 1850 was very active in the Democratic politics of that state.[143] He was a loyal supporter of James Buchanan, as is shown by the large amount of correspondence between them. Ward was also connected with national Democratic affairs. In 1852 he was a member of the Democratic National Committee, and in 1856 he was made chairman of that committee.[144]   Ward was connected with P. A. Hargous before the latter secured possession of the Garay grant. In 1846 he requested Buchanan, then Secretary of State, to send certain United States Treasury reports to P. A. Hargous, and promised to give Buchanan his reason at a later time for this request.[145]   At the time he was sent to Mexico, he was the agent and counselor for the claimants under the Garay grant.[146]

In view of the connection of Ward with the Garay grant, and the decision of President Pierce not to press that grant, it appears strange that Ward was selected as the special messenger to Mexico.  The New York *Tribune* at a later date, explained the appointment of Ward as a move of the Garay claimants to secure indemnification, as they realized the futility of any hope of aid from Gadsden.[147]   This paper also declared that Sidney Webster, private secretary to President Pierce, was the chief conspirator, and that

---

[142] See map. No. 2, page 92.

[143] A large portion of the correspondence of Ward is in the Buchanan Papers at the Historical Society of Pennsylvania.

[144] Ward to Buchanan, June 28, 1856, Buchanan Papers.

[145] *Ibid.* to *ibid.*, Feb. 16, 1846, *ibid.*

[146] N. Y. *Times*, Jan. 11, 1854.

[147] N. Y. *Tribune*, Apr. 13, 1854.

President Pierce had been led into a trap. A correspondent of a southern newspaper also made the charge that intimate friends of President Pierce, agents of Hargous, had influenced him to send Ward to Mexico.[148] The New York *Times* said that President Pierce knew of the connection of Ward with the Garay grant, and had forbidden him to mention that subject in Mexico.[149] The actions of Ward in Mexico, in favor of the Garay grant, seem to indicate the existence of some scheme by which Ward was appointed. On the other hand, the appointment may have been nothing more than a reward for his faithful services in the political campaign of the previous year.

The mission of Ward to Mexico was kept secret from the public. To his friend Buchanan, Ward mentioned only that he would be absent on a journey for a period of a few weeks.[150] He arrived in Mexico City on November 11, 1854.[151] On December 4, he informed Marcy that in order to gather more material for the Department of State, he had decided to extend his stay in Mexico until the departure of the next mail packet.[152] He used his time, however, in an effort to have an indemnity for the Garay claimants written into the treaty with Mexico.

Immediately upon his arrival in Mexico City, Ward, communicated his instructions to Gadsden. He communicated all that he had been authorized to report and in addition he demanded that Gadsden include in any negotiation a large indemnity for the Garay grantees. Of his demands, Gadsden informed Marcy that, "indeed, to hear Mr. Ward talk and seemingly under the confidential

[148] Augusta *Daily Chronicle and Sentinel*, Apr. 18, 1854.

[149] N. Y. *Times*, Jan. 17, 1854.

[150] Ward to Buchanan, Oct. 22, 1853, Buchanan Papers.

[151] Ward to Marcy, Nov. 18, 1853, Marcy Papers, vol. 44.

[152] *Ibid.* to *ibid.*, Dec. 4, 1853, Dept. of State, Special Agents, C. L. Ward, Package.

cloak of a private messenger you might suppose my mission was for the Garay grant."[153]  He refused to trust Ward, and compelled him to furnish the instructions in written form.  This Ward reluctantly did, in a lengthy letter of November 14.[154]  He represented to Gadsden that the Sloo concession had not been accepted by President Pierce as a substitute for the Garay grant, and that the latter was still upheld by the administration.  Only the supposed situation in Mexico, which demanded speedy action, Ward informed Gadsden, had influenced President Pierce not to demand indemnity for the claimants in the treaty.  The present situation in Mexico, Ward continued, would now warrant such action, which would be consonant with the views and wishes of President Pierce.  Gadsden was warned by Ward, that "a treaty simply securing new territory or a new route for a railway which has its rivals and opponents in various forms; in other words, a treaty looking solely to the speculative interests of the country instead of the country, and paying large sums to promote them, while long pending and real injuries of individuals are left unmolested," would never receive the approval of the administration or the citizens of the United States.

With reluctance Gadsden accepted Ward's statements, but to Marcy he expressed his disgust at such diplomatic procedure.  He was sure that President Pierce did not entertain the views, reported by Ward in regard to the Garay grant.  He declared that if $5,000,000 was to be deducted for the "cormorant appetite of Ward and Co.," and $3,000,000 for legitimate and urgent private claims,

---

[153] Gadsden to Marcy, Nov. 20, 1853, Dept. of State, Des., Mex., vol. 18, private.

[154] Ward to Gadsden, Nov. 14, 1853, Dept. of State, Special Agents, C. L. Ward, Package.

treaty negotiations might as well be abandoned.[155]   But, in obedience to Ward's alleged instructions, Gadsden demanded of the Mexican government indemnity for the Garay grantees, and in the treaty concluded, there was an article to that effect.  The statements of Ward in regard to the Garay grant were disavowed by Secretary Marcy.  He wrote Gadsden that "Ward was directed to inform you, not to embarrass your negotiations with it."[156]

The negotiation of a treaty after the arrival of Ward involved a struggle between Gadsden on one side and Ward and his associates on the other as to who should influence the Mexican negotiators.  There were many hindrances to the successful negotiation of a treaty.  One of the most important of these was the filibustering expedition of William Walker of November, 1853, into Lower California.[157]  With less than fifty men, he made a lodgement at La Paz, and proclaimed Lower California an independent republic.[158]  This act was inopportune for the negotiation of a treaty by Gadsden, for it further convinced Santa Anna that the United States intended to annex the remainder of the Mexican territory.[159]  Protests were made by the Mexican government both to Gadsden and to Marcy.[160]  Gadsden at once sent instructions to the American consuls on the western coast of Mexico and to the commanders of American war vessels on the Pacific to intercept the

[155] Gadsden to Marcy, Nov. 20, 1853, Dept. of State, Des., Mex., vol. 18, private.

[156] Marcy to Gadsden, Dec. 22, 1853, Dept. of State, Inst., Mex., vol. 16, no. 19.

[157] A good account of Walker's expedition is in Scroggs, W. O., *Filibusters and Financiers*, 31–51.

[158] Proclamation of Walker, in N. Y. *Times*, Jan. 5, 1854.

[159] Doyle to Clarendon, Dec. 9, 1853, F. O., Mex., vol. 261, no. 117, secret.

[160] Almonte to Marcy, Dec. 21, 1853, Dept. of State, Notes to Dept., Mex. Leg., vol. 7.

raid.[161] W. H. Aspinwall, of the Pacific Mail Steamship Line, offered to capture Walker, because of his adverse influence on the negotiation of a treaty with Mexico.[162] Ward, who had just arrived in Mexico when the news of Walker's expedition had come, informed Marcy that it would embarrass the negotiations of Gadsden with Santa Anna.[163] Gadsden informed the Charleston *Daily Courier* that the peninsula of California would probably have been obtained by further negotiation, "had not the insane expedition caused Santa Anna to set his face resolutely against it." [164]

Santa Anna believed that the American government entertained sinister motives toward Mexico. The Mexican press, controlled by Santa Anna, was hostile to the United States. *El Orden* declared that the hostile attacks of America upon Mexico, through her filibustering raids, Tehuantepec policy, and public press, were so atrocious and barbarous that they could not be exaggerated.[165] Santa Anna turned to the European powers for aid to restrain the ambitious designs of the United States. Circulars to this effect were sent to the Mexican diplomatic agents in England, France, and Spain.[166] A claims convention was made with Spain in 1853, to ally her with Mexico against the United States.[167] An offensive and defensive alliance with Spain was proposed by Santa Anna, for mutual assistance

[161] Gadsden to Marcy, Nov. 18, 1853, Dept. of State, Des., Mex., vol. 18, no. 13.

[162] Aspinwall to Dandridge, Dec. 18, 1853, Marcy Papers, vol. 45.

[163] Ward to Marcy, Nov. 18, 1853, *ibid.*, vol. 44.

[164] Charleston *Daily Courier*, Jan. 21, 1854.

[165] From N. O. *Daily Picayune*, July 16, 1853.

[166] Bolton, H. E., *Guide to Materials for the History of the United States in the Principal Archives of Mexico*, 229-230.

[167] Cripps to Marcy, June 19, 1856, Dept. of State, Des., Mex., vol. 19, no. 92.

against American attacks on Cuba and Mexico.[168]  From observations dropped by the Emperor of the French to the Mexican minister at Paris, Santa Anna believed that France would support Mexico against American inroads.[169]

It was to Great Britain, however, that Santa Anna looked especially for aid against the United States and he demanded some promise to that effect from the British minister, Doyle. The notes of Gadsden to Secretary Bonilla were immediately sent to Doyle, to be transmitted to the British Foreign Office.[170]  To Doyle he pictured the hostile attitude of America toward Mexico and the attempt of Gadsden to purchase half of the Mexican domain.[171] Santa Anna pointed out to Doyle the great damage to British commerce that would result from the acquisition of the Mexican territory by the United States. He hoped that Great Britain would take the lead to preserve the balance of power in America, and he offered to resign his position to any foreign prince who would be supported on the Mexican throne by the European powers.[172]  Doyle gave Santa Anna no hope that such a proposition would be entertained because, as he informed the Earl of Clarendon, the British Foreign Secretary, he did not believe in the sincerity of Santa Anna. Instead, he advised Santa Anna to arrange his finances and to avoid conflict with the United States.[173] Clarendon declared that intervention in the internal affairs of a country was contrary to the practice of

[168] Doyle to Clarendon, Dec. 3, 1853, F. O., Mex., vol. 261, no. 117, secret.
[169] *Ibid.*
[170] *Ibid.* to *ibid.*, Dec. 18, 1853, *ibid.*, vol. 261, no. 120, secret.
[171] *Ibid. to ibid.*, Dec. 3, 1853, *ibid.*, vol. 261, no. 117, secret.
[172] *Ibid.*
[173] *Ibid.*

Great Britain and that such intervention in Mexico would be resented by the United States.[174]

Gadsden lacked many of the requisites of a successful diplomat, and his boisterous manner did not aid the negotiation of a treaty. He was regarded in Mexico as a true disciple of Andrew Jackson, with an inflexible and determined will for whatever he considered right.[175] He explained to Buchanan that he had no great talent for diplomatic technique but that he relied on "the straight-forward direction of a novice in diplomacy, by striking boldly at the truth and leaving the rest to Providence."[176] As he had no respect for Santa Anna and his autocratic system of government, he became very arrogant in his relations with the Mexican officials. Complaints were made by the Mexican government of his hostile attitude, and American citizens in Mexico were asked to induce Gadsden to change his diplomatic tactics.[177] The unfriendly attitude of Gadsden during the negotiation was one reason for the later demand by the Mexican government for his recall.

In order to maintain his rule, Santa Anna was forced to make a treaty with the United States which involved the sale of Mexican territory. There was no hope of assistance from the European nations in case of a war with the United States, and Santa Anna knew that such a war, single-handed, meant his downfall. Conditions were such in Mexico that financial assistance was needed, as all attempts to secure an additional revenue through forced loans and high tariffs had failed. A revolution was in progress which threatened to overthrow the government unless an army was immediately equipped, and that meant

---

[174] Foreign Office to Doyle, Jan. 16, 1854, *ibid.*, vol. 265, no. 9. confidential.

[175] N. O. *Daily Picayune*, Dec. 13, 1853.

[176] Gadsden to Buchanan, Oct. 3, 1853, Buchanan Papers.

[177] N. O. *Daily Picayune*, Dec. 26, 1853.

the need of much money.  To secure this money and to avoid a war, Santa Anna was forced to negotiate a treaty with the United States.  In a manifesto in 1855, he justified the treaty and the sale of Mexican territory because it avoided another war with the United States, "at a time when the treasury was empty and the nation in the midst of the horrors of anarchy." [178]  Bonilla thought it better to sell a small portion of valueless territory than to risk the loss of all in a war with the United States.[179]

Despite Gadsden's protests, Santa Anna refused to treat except on the basis of line No. 5, which gave the United States only enough territory for a railroad route.  A commission, composed of Secretary Bonilla and two engineers, was appointed by Santa Anna to negotiate with Gadsden.[180] When he was informed that such a commission would be appointed, Gadsden addressed a lengthy note to Bonilla on November 29, in which he made an earnest plea for a negotiation with route No. 1. as the basis.[181]  He pointed out that "the spirit of the age" would ultimately cause the northern states of Mexico to unite with the United States. Such a cession, he asserted, would enable Mexico to consolidate her strength in the more populous and richer states.  He later agreed to the Mexican selection of line No. 5, but declared that no treaty on those limits could be more than a temporary expedient.[182]

At the first meeting of the commission, December 10, 1853, a tentative treaty was presented by Gadsden, which

---

[178] *Manifesto del Presidente de la República a la Nación, 1855.*
[179] Doyle to Clarendon, Jan. 2, 1855, F. O., Mex., vol. 276, no. 1.
[180] Bonilla to Gadsden, Nov. 30, 1853, Dept. of State, Des., Mex., vol. 18, with no. 15.
[181] Gadsden to Bonilla, Nov. 29, 1853, *ibid.*
[182] *Ibid.* to *ibid.*, Dec. 3, 1853, *ibid.*

was accepted as a basis of discussion.[183]   On December 16,
a second conference was held, but in this meeting, the two
sets of commissioners differed widely as to the amount of
land to be ceded and the amount of money to be paid for
the same.   Gadsden informed Marcy that the communications of Almonte from Washington, and the influence of
speculators in Indian claims, were responsible for the
large demands of Mexico.[184]

The next conference was on December 22, but before
that date, Gadsden had made an offer through a note to
Bonilla for the purchase of Lower California.   To this proposal Bonilla replied in the meeting that he had no power
to alienate that portion of the Mexican territory, and that
only in view of the imperative need of land for a railroad,
did Mexico agree to cede any territory to the United States.
Bonilla then outlined a boundary between the two countries, which was discussed and referred to the next meeting.

On December 23, much progress was made by the commissioners in the negotiation of the treaty.   Except for a
few changes to insure a railroad route, Gadsden agreed to
the boundary line designated by Bonilla.   The articles
of the treaty of Guadalupe Hidalgo, which promised protection to the civil and ecclesiastical rights and property
of the inhabitants in the ceded territory were continued in
the new treaty.   It was decided that one commissioner from
each country should run the boundary line, which when
established was to be a part of the treaty.   Bonilla offered
to release the United States from article XI, provided that
Mexico was compensated for the losses which the government and citizens had suffered in the past from the Indian
depredations, and for the obligations which Mexico would

[183] ''Notes of Diplomatic Conferences for the Adjustment of
Various Issues between the United States and Mexico, Dec. 1853,''
*ibid.*, vol. 18.   The information in regard to the work of the commission is derived from this document.

[184] Gadsden to Marcy, Dec. 16, 1853, *ibid.*, vol. 18, no. 16.

naturally assume by the abrogation of the article. Gadsden refused to accept such an interpretation of the article,
but proposed, as a compromise, the entire relinquishment
of the article by Mexico, which act would be considered in
the amount he was authorized to pay for the arrangement
of all the issues between Mexico and the United States.

In the session of December 24, the remainder of the disputed issues were settled. To the demand of Gadsden for
the recognition by Mexico of the Garay grant, Bonilla replied that this concession was considered invalid by the
present Mexican government. He thought that the only
way to dispose of the matter was to include it within the
claims of the American citizens against Mexico, which were
to be assumed by the United States. This proposal was accepted by Gadsden, and although the Garay claimants alone
demanded indemnity of $5,000,000, the latter sum was
designated for all the American claims against Mexico.
For all the concessions by Mexico, Gadsden offered the sum
of $12,000,000. Bonilla refused to accept this offer, and
it was finally decided that the United States should pay
$15,000,000 to Mexico, and in addition, assume to the ex-
tent of $5,000,000, the private claims of its citizens against
Mexico. At the suggestion of Bonilla, an additional article was included which stated that both governments should
give their mutual aid of naval and military forces for the
suppression of lawless incursions into their respective
territories.

The contents of the treaty as concluded were as
follows:[185]

ARTICLE I.      — The new boundary line (shown as
                line No. 7 on map).

ARTICLE II.     — Abrogation by Mexico of article XI
                of the treaty of Guadalupe Hidalgo,

[185] *S. Ex. Journal*, X, 312–315: N. O. *Daily Picayune*, Feb. 22,
1853.

ARTICLE III.
but a promise on the part of the United States to aid Mexico against these Indians.
— Payment by the United States to Mexico of $15,000,000 and the assumption of all American claims against Mexico, "including the claim of the so-called Garay, whose lawful existence Mexico does not recognize."

ARTICLE IV. — Organization of the claims commission.

ARTICLE V. — Navigation by the United States, of the Gulf of California, the Colorado and Brazos rivers not to be interrupted.

ARTICLE VI. — Reaffirmation of the provisions of articles VIII, IX, XVI, and XVII of the treaty of Guadalupe Hidalgo.

ARTICLE VII. — Recognition of the Mexican land grants in the ceded territory.

ARTICLE VIII.— Promise of mutual coöperation to suppress filibustering expeditions.

ARTICLE IX. — Reaffirmation of articles XXI and XXII of the treaty of Guadalupe Hidalgo.

ARTICLE X. — Ratification of the treaty.

On December 30, the commissioners met at the American legation, where the treaty was signed. At the request of Gadsden, it was agreed that the stipulations of the treaty were to be kept secret until the treaty was ratified. The commission then adjourned, "after mutual congratulations upon the result of their many conferences, so often threatened by the intrigues of speculators and persons interested in preventing a happy understanding between the two countries.''

Congratulations were indeed in order, for during the negotiation of the treaty Gadsden had been constantly hindered by outside interests composed of both American and Mexican speculators and claimants. Gadsden had early found his work to be onerous because of the multiplicity of private claims which, he asserted, increased in a geometrical ratio.[186] Speculators in Indian claims exerted their influence to secure an indemnity in the treaty for their claims.[187] The professional treaty makers of Mexico offered to negotiate a treaty for Gadsden on condition that they be well rewarded.[188] The remarks of Robert J. Walker in favor of the southern railroad route through the territory desired by Gadsden and his statement that Gadsden was instructed to purchase a right of way at any price were reported by Almonte to Santa Anna.[189] Such rumors increased the demands of Santa Anna. ''Thus,'' declared the Charleston *Daily Courier,* ''does the spirit of American speculation mar our negotiations abroad as it does at home.'' [190]

Secretary Marcy considered Almonte responsible for the circulation of erroneous statements which embarrassed Gadsden's negotiations. In an interview with Almonte, he assured him that ''any idea that the United States would give an enormous sum for a trail of barren country in that region ought at once to be abandoned by his government, as also the idea that a cession of such a tract was not to be accompanied by an adjustment of claims for damages

---

[186] Gadsden to Marcy, Aug. 31, 1853, Dept. of State, Des., Mex., vol. 18, no. 2.

[187] *Ibid.* to *ibid.,* Dec. 16, 1853, *ibid.,* vol. 18, no. 16.

[188] *Ibid.* to *ibid.,* Oct. 3, 1853, *ibid.,* vol. 18, private.

[189] Charleston *Daily Courier,* Jan. 25, 1854.

[190] *Ibid.*

arising under the treaty of Guadalupe Hidalgo.'' [191]   Marcy
hoped that Mexico would not ''permit herself to be misled
by the speculative views'' of persons who had no connection with public affairs.   Almonte denied that he had
influenced the negotiations, but suggested that the negotiation had been delayed and hindered by the demand of the
American government for the large tracts of land.   Marcy
replied that, ''beyond a feasible route for a railroad, it was
not territory that was wanted, but a safe and easily defended boundary  .  .  .   and in having such a boundary,
Mexico was much more interested than the United
States.'' [192]

Speculation by private claimants was small in compari-
son with the attempt of the Garay grantees to have inserted
into the treaty a large indemnity for their losses.   Ward,
in league with Escandon, a leading Mexican speculator,
attempted to put in an article whereby the Garay grantees
would be definitely granted an indemnity of $3,000,000.[193]
The reports of Gadsden to Marcy place Ward in an unfavorable light.   On January 2, 1854, he wrote about the
''extraordinary movements by Hargous, Ward, and Co.''
to defeat the treaty.[194]   Their hostility to him, because he
had foiled them, was so bitter that he feared that they would
prevent him from securing a place on the boat to America.
As to the treaty, he wrote: ''This is said to be the only
treaty for years which has ever been concluded without
'Brokerage,' a Mexican signification, where the broker
greazes the officials and retains all the tallow .... W. . . '.
instincts were too strong to resist.'' [195]   Later in 1855,
when Hargous and Ward attempted, as a means of revenge,
to have Gadsden removed from his position as minister,

---

[191] Marcy to Gadsden, Jan. 6, 1854, Dept. of State, Inst., Mex., vol. 16, no. 20.

[192] *Ibid.*

the latter divulged more of the secret diplomacy. He declared that had he not penetrated the intrigue, a provision would have been inserted in the treaty for an indemnity of $3,000,000 for Hargous, in which Escandon, Santa Anna, and Ward would have participated.[196] Ward attempted to influence the negotiations through the agency of the Mexican negotiators. A letter written by Ward to Bonilla was seen by Gadsden which showed how Ward had profited by a brief residence in Mexico City.[197] It was the discovery of a letter written by Ward to a Mexican commissioner that later occasioned the investigation of the Ward intrigue by the United States Senate.

Gadsden was much pleased with his treaty, because he had secured a territory that contained valuable mineral resources.[198] He declared that all issues between the United States and Mexico were reconciled on conditions honorable and just to both countries.[199] After the negotiation of the treaty, Gadsden returned to the United States. He arrived in New Orleans on January 12, 1854. In answer to interrogations from the custom-house official, Gadsden proudly replied: "Sir, I am General Gadsden. There is nothing in my trunk but my treaty." [200]

Thus, Gadsden had accomplished the important task of his mission to Mexico. The boundary line dispute was settled by the purchase of additional Mexican territory by the United States. An eligible railroad route to the Pacific

---

[193] Gadsden to Marcy, July 11, 1855, Dept. of State, Des., Mex., vol. 19, Unofficial.

[194] *Ibid.* to *ibid.*, Jan. 2, 1854, Marcy Papers, vol. 46.

[195] *Ibid.*

[196] *Ibid.* to *ibid.*, July 11, 1855, Dept. of State, Des., Mex., vol. 19, Unofficial.

[197] *Ibid.*

[198] *Ibid.* to *ibid.*, Jan. 12, 1854, Marcy Papers, vol. 47.

[199] *Ibid.* to *ibid.*, Jan. 15, 1854, *ibid.*

[200] N. Y. *Herald*, Jan. 30, 1854.

on American soil was secured by the treaty. The isthmian question was partially settled by the grant of an indemnity to the Garay claimants for their losses. In spite of a hostile government, outside influences, and constant opposition, a treaty favorable to both nations had been negotiated.

The treaty had now to face President Pierce and the United States Senate for ratification. Despite the precautions of Gadsden to keep secret the contents of the treaty, the negotiation of a treaty was reported in the United States before Gadsden reached New Orleans, and on January 20, a day after Gadsden arrived in Charleston, the gist of the treaty was before the public.

# CHAPTER V

From September, 1853, to January, 1854, the American newspapers except for a few speculative statements, were, almost silent in regard to the negotiation of a treaty with Mexico. The mission of Ward to Mexico had been successfully concealed from the press. Consequently, the report of the New York *Herald* on January 4, 1854, that a new treaty with Mexico had been concluded, caused considerable comment from the other newspapers.[1] As this report was published only five days after the treaty had been signed, the New York *Herald* evidently based its statement upon generalities rather than upon any particular facts. The mouthpiece of the administration, the Washington *Union,* at once replied with a denial that a treaty had been made.[2] The New York *Times* also declared the statement of the *Herald* to be a fabrication, and suggested that the information of the *Herald* was based on some speculative remarks published a few days before in the *Times.*[3] At any rate the *expose* of the *Herald* set the other newspapers to discussing and speculating concerning the treaty.

Certainly the *Herald* had some source of inside information, for on January 20, 1854, the day after Ward arrived in Washington with the treaty, a gist of the treaty was published by this paper, which corresponded

[1] N. Y. *Herald,* Jan. 4, 1854.
[2] Washington *Union,* Jan. 7, 1854.
[3] N. Y. *Times,* Jan. 7, 1854.

almost exactly with the official document.[4]  The *Herald* began at once to attack the treaty.  The administration, and in particular, Secretary Marcy, was defamed and ridiculed for the negotiation of such a treaty.  Marcy declared to a friend, that "the New York *Herald* has abused me, from the date of its establishment down to the present time."[5]  He criticized Buchanan for his belief in what the *Herald* published, for, as he wrote, "where it is known, it is a very harmless sheet."[6]  The New York *Times* informed its readers that "truth and the *Herald's* correspondents have not been on speaking terms for months."[7]  For the political scandal of this period, the *Herald* is a good informant.

With the contents of the treaty before the public, the press began to take sides on the question.  The northern papers with a few exceptions, such as the New York *Times*, began to criticize the treaty.  Their opposition was based on partisan or sectional reasons.  A few southern papers criticized the treaty because they considered it a poor bargain.  The New Orleans *Daily Picayune* informed its readers that as the territory purchased was only wild land, it was "not much to felicitate ourselves upon."[8]  Another declared the few million acres of worthless land to be poor enough to bankrupt the owner.[9]  A Tennessee paper was not enthusiastic over the treaty because it gave money to Santa Anna to build up a South American Confederation hostile to the United States.[10]

[4] N. Y. *Herald*, Jan. 20, 1854.
[5] Marcy to Belmont, Nov. 5, 1854, Marcy Papers, Private letter-book.
[6] Marcy to Mason, Dec. 31, 1854, *ibid.*
[7] N. Y. *Times*, Jan. 11, 1854.
[8] N. O. *Daily Picayune*, Jan. 18, 1854.
[9] Santa Fé *Weekly Gazette*, Apr. 1, 1854.
[10] Memphis *Daily Eagle and Enquirer*, Mar. 30, 1854.

Except for a few such criticisms, the newspapers of the South praised the treaty. The New York *Times* also became an ardent supporter of it. The *Times* favored the treaty because it settled all the pending issues with Mexico.[11] The Washington *Union* declared that it saved America from a war, for since Mexico would not yield the Mesilla valley, the only alternative "was to unsheath the sword."[12] Peaceful acquisition, even at high prices, the Savannah *Republican* considered better in the long run and much cheaper than conquests.[13] The release of the United States from article XI, the settlement of the isthmian question, and the acquisition of cheap land were also subjects of congratulation. The New York *Times* advised the Senate to accept the treaty, and warned that unless it were ratified, France or England would secure the isthmian connection. "Such an arrangement," it declared, "would cost us our Pacific possessions should we happen to get into war with France or England before our Pacific Railroad is completed."[14] The Mobile *Register* went so far as to declare the treaty to be the most important ever negotiated by the United States.[15]

Gadsden received both praise and criticism for his work. The Mobile *Register* was certain that the success of the negotiation was due to the "honorable frankness of the American diplomat."[16] The Charleston *Daily Courier* was lavish in its praise of the diplomacy of Gadsden. It predicted that he would be called to a higher position, that "in event of certain rumored changes in the Cabinet taking place, General Gadsden is mentioned in connection

[11] N. Y. *Times*, Mar. 27, 1854.
[12] Washington *Union*, Mar. 28, 1854.
[13] Savannah *Daily Republican*, Jan. 25, 1854.
[14] N. Y. *Times*, Apr. 7, 1854.
[15] From Nashville *Daily Union and American*, Jan. 26, 1854.
[16] *Ibid.*

with the Treasury Department . . . for which as well as the War Department he is eminently qualified." [17] Even the New York *Herald* was compelled to praise his efficiency. It admitted that "it is but right that justice should be rendered to the negotiator of the treaty. . . . Mr. Gadsden is the only one of our foreign envoys who from the first devoted himself thoroughly and in a statesmanlike manner in the discharge of the duties of his office." [18]

On the other hand, the northern papers attacked Gadsden. The Philadelphia *Public Ledger* described him as a filibuster and nullifier and a poor selection on the part of President Pierce to treat with Santa Anna.[19] The Baltimore *Sun* accused him of disobedience to his instructions.[20] To the statement of the Mobile *Register* that Gadsden had "talents of a high order, cultivated and refined by education and a keen perception of human action," the New York *Herald* replied that the only keen perception General Gadsden had was the perception that Santa Anna wanted money, and Santa Anna had the same perception that James Gadsden wanted a certain strip of wild land.[21]

Jefferson Davis was denounced by some northern papers as the master hand behind the whole negotiation. In an article entitled, "The Secret History of the Gadsden Treaty," the New York *Herald* made the following charges :[22]

1. The treaty had its origin in the fertile imagination of Jefferson Davis.

[17] Charleston *Daily Courier*, Jan. 21, 1854.
[18] From Charleston *Daily Courier*, Jan. 21, 1854.
[19] Phila. *Public Ledger*, Jan. 30, 1854.
[20] From N. Y. *Herald*, Jan. 19, 1854.
[21] N. Y. *Herald*, Jan. 20, 1854.
[22] *Ibid.*, Jan. 30, 1854.

2. Gadsden was interested in the connection of Charles-ton by an air line railroad with the port of San Diego.

3. Jefferson Davis owned land near the boundaries of Louisiana and Texas, which were to quadruple in value by their contiguity to the Great Pacific Railroad.

4. Through the influence of Davis, Gadsden had been appointed minister to Mexico.

5. Davis had the treaty negotiated to kill Benton, who hurt the presidential aspirations of Davis through his central railroad scheme.

The Washington *Union* defended Davis, with a declaration that he had inherited no piece of property, nor held a foot of land, capable of enhancement by the southern railroad to the Pacific Ocean.[23]

The treaty was praised by southern papers because it secured a route for a southern transcontinental railroad. The Texas *State Gazette* declared that the treaty cleared the way for the construction of the Pacific railroad over the most practicable and shortest route.[24]  The treaty was also favored in Tennessee because it gave the Union the shortest route, and a route which would "naturally and easily connect with the Tennessee railroad improvements."[25]  It was pointed out that the route designated by General Gadsden at the Memphis Convention in 1845 would be embraced in the cession of Mexican territory.[26]

On the other hand this aid to a southern railroad was not relished in the northern states.  The New York *Herald* charged that the treaty was a result of the instructions of the Southern Pacific Coalition, headed by the Davis and Cushing section of the cabinet.[27]  The Philadelphia *Pub-*

---

[23] Washington *Union*, Mar. 9, 1854.
[24] Texas *State Gazette*, Mar. 28, 1854.
[25] Nashville *Daily Union and American*, Feb. 5, 1854.
[26] Charleston *Daily Courier*, Jan. 21, 1854.
[27] N. Y. *Herald*, Feb. 7, 1854.

*lic Ledger* declared that the treaty might as well be called, "a purchase of the right of way for a railroad to the Pacific," as any other name.[28]   The New York *Tribune* demanded the expenditure of a few million dollars on the rivers and harbors of the North before millions were paid for a southern railroad.[29]

As the slavery question was before the country in the form of the Kansas-Nebraska bill, it was natural that the purchase of Mexican territory should be denounced by northern men as another scheme for the increase of slave territory.   The Philadelphia *Public Ledger* declared that the treaty would again bring up the slavery question.[30] The New York *Herald* said that it would add several slave states to the Union, and thus give preponderance to the South in the national council.   "Such a course," it continued, "may well cause President Pierce, Mr. Marcy and other Wilmot Proviso conspirators to pause, hesitate and tremble."[31]   Horace Greely wrote, "The Gadsden Treaty gives $10,000,000 to Santa Anna for a large body of territory and for the abrogation of the foolish article in the treaty of Guadalupe Hidalgo worth about $2,000,000, . . . leaving $8,000,000 to be paid for controverting territory now free into slave territory, or that the most earnest supporters of the treaty mean shall become such."[32]

Some southern writers favored the treaty because it secured more slave territory.   An advocate of the treaty wrote in a southern journal that if the North rejected the treaty, the Mexican government would then be destroyed. The southern and southwestern people, he argued, would

---

[28] Phila. *Public Ledger,* Apr. 11, 1854.
[29] N. Y. *Tribune,* Apr. 28, 1854.
[30] From N. Y. *Herald,* Jan. 19, 1854.
[31] N. Y. *Herald,* Jan. 16, 1854.
[32] N. Y. *Tribune,* Apr. 28, 1854.

then be obliged to take Mexico upon their hands, and "the shortsighted policy of the North will be the means of creating slaveholding communities in all Spanish North America from El Paso to the Gulf of Darien."[33]   The Charleston *Mercury* warned the southern senators that the ratification of the treaty was "in all probability the last chance to recover a single step of the many lost; and that holding the fate of their country in their hands, they were called upon to decide not a point of expediency, but a principle and an interest affecting all that Southern people hold dear, their rights, their property and their social safety."[34]   The New York *Times,* in a reply to the papers which opposed the treaty because it annexed more slave territory, declared: "Admit that it does so, what then? Will not a war result in the absorption of ten times the amount received by the treaty?"[35]

C. L. Ward arrived in Washington, January 19, 1854, and immediately presented the treaty to President Pierce.[36] The inclusion in the treaty of stipulations not authorized by the President created an excitement at the White House.[37]   A cabinet meeting was held on the same day and for almost a month the treaty was continually discussed in the cabinet.[38]   The treaty was unsatisfactory to the President because he was unwilling to favor either the Garay or the Sloo grant.   As shown later in his message in regard to the Conkling convention, he favored a policy of governmental aloofness in support of private interests in foreign countries.[39]

[33] From N. Y. *Tribune,* Apr. 13, 1854.
[34] From N. Y. *Times,* Jan. 25, 1854.
[35] N. Y. *Times,* Mar. 27, 1854.
[36] N. Y. *Herald,* Jan. 20, 1854.
[37] N.Y. *Tribune,* Apr. 13, 1854.
[38] N. Y. *Herald,* Feb. 9, 1854.
[39] *S. Ex. Journal,* IX, 235–236.

On the question of the acceptance of the treaty, the cabinet was divided. It was reported that Cushing, Marcy, Davis, and Dobbin were in favor of submitting the treaty to the Senate for advice as to its ratification, while President Pierce, McClelland and Campbell advised the rejection of it.[40] Guthrie was said to be neutral. President Pierce, although he was much opposed to the treaty, finally agreed to submit it to the Senate, with the recommendation of such amendments as would make the treaty acceptable to him.[41] In this decision he was greatly influenced by Senator Rusk, of Texas, who earnestly advocated the acceptance of the treaty by the President.[42]

Consequently, on February 10, President Pierce sent the treaty to the Senate for advice as to its ratification, accompanied by a message which recommended three changes therein.[43] He advised that the obligation of the United States, under article II, to rescue and to return to Mexico the goods and captives taken by the American Indians be made reciprocal. He rejected article III, by which the United States assumed the claims of its citizens against Mexico, with the special designation of the claims of the Garay grantees. He recommended instead, an article that agreed to assume the claims, but without any special mention of the claims under the Garay grant. Article VIII was changed by Pierce from a promise of mutual coöperation with Mexico to suppress filibustering expeditions to a general stipulation that the United States would cheerfully coöperate with Mexico in the suppression of all unlawful invasions on both sides of the boundary line.

The proceedings of the Senate in regard to the treaty

[40] N. Y. *Herald*, Feb. 9, 1854.
[41] Washington *Union*, Apr. 9, 1854.
[42] N. Y. *Journal of Commerce*, Feb. 13, 1854.
[43] *S. Ex. Journal*, IX, 238–239.

were held in executive sessions. The secret sessions however, did not prove effective, for as the Washington *Union* said, "the proceedings are only nominally secret." [44] All the leading newspapers printed an account of the debates in the Senate, and upon those reports, in addition to the *Senate Executive Journal*, is based the story of the ratification of the treaty by the Senate. The treaty and the message of President Pierce had been sent to the Senate in confidence, but within a short time the treaty was printed in the newspapers.[45] This caused the Senate to appoint a committee to investigate the means by which the treaty was made public.[46] The senators were interrogated as to the publication of the treaty, but all declared their innocence in the matter.[47] The New York *Herald* was especially obnoxious to the Senate and on February 17, a motion was made to arrest the editor for the printing of the treaty and other matter as a contempt of the Senate.[48]

The treaty was sent to the Senate on February 10, but it was not considered by that body until March 13.[49] This delay was due to the debate on the Kansas-Nebraska bill and to the absence of Senator Mason, chairman of the Committee on Foreign Relations.[50] On February 13, the Senate confirmed the appointment of Gadsden as minister to Mexico. Only two senators, Houston, of Texas, and Thompson, of Kentucky, opposed this action.[51] On March 9, the treaty was reported from the Committee on Foreign

[44] Washington *Union*, Apr. 9, 1854.
[45] Phila. *North American*, Feb. 15, 1854.
[46] *S. Ex. Journal*, IX, 247.
[47] *Ibid.*, 272.
[48] N. Y. *Herald*, Feb. 18, 1854.
[49] *S. Ex. Journal*, IX, 264.
[50] Washington *Union*, Mar. 7, 1854.
[51] *S. Ex. Journal*, IX, 241.

Relations.[52] All of the proposed amendments of President Pierce were accepted by the committee except that in regard to article III. The committee retained the special mention of the Garay claims within the American claims against Mexico. Just and proper indemnity was to be given the holders of the Garay grant, but it was not "to include compensation for any loss of anticipated profits." [53] This report in favor of the Garay claimants was made by a committee composed of Senators Mason, of Virginia, Douglas, of Illinois, Slidell, of Louisiana, Weller, of California, Clayton, of Delaware, and Everett, of Massachusetts.[54]

Before the action of the Senate in regard to the treaty is discussed, the many difficulties which faced its ratification should be mentioned. In the first place, the treaty was sent to the Senate at a very inopportune time. Northern Senators, embittered by the Kansas-Nebraska bill, saw in the Gadsden treaty only an acquisition of more slave territory and a route for a southern railroad to the Pacific. The same senators who fought Douglas's bill so violently took up the fight against the Gadsden treaty. This coterie of Foot, Seward, Sumner, Fish, Chase, Wade, Walker, Hamlin and Fessenden, furnished the nucleus of opposition to the treaty. To them the acquisition of territory, however small, wherein slavery might be countenanced was a national crime, and should therefore be opposed.

On the other hand, the small amount of territory acquired was a cause for the opposition on the part of some senators to the treaty. Senators Gwin and Weller, of California, declared that they could not support the

---

[52] *Ibid.*, 261–262.

[53] *Ibid.*, 262.

[54] *Cong. Globe*, 33 Cong., 1 sess. (1853–1854), XXVIII, pt. 1, p. 27.

treaty unless the boundary line were extended southward to the twenty-seventh parallel of north latitude.[55]   They desired this extension of the boundary line so as to secure a mountain barrier between the two countries, a port on the Gulf of California, and the possession of the mines of Sonora.[56]   Before the treaty was sent to the Senate, Senator Gwin announced that he would oppose it to the last point, unless it were materially amended, and throughout the process of ratification his attitude was hostile to the treaty.[57]   Other ultra-southerners desired enough Mexican territory to make a slave state, so as to offset the free state of California.[58]

The struggle between the Garay and Sloo grantees added another hindrance to ratification.   The Sloo people declared that unless some compromise was made with them, they would move heaven and earth to defeat the treaty.[59] Some recognition of the Sloo grant was made a *sine qua non* for ratification by Clayton, of Delaware, and Bell, of Tennessee.[60]   The proceedings of the Senate, at times, resembled more a fight between the friends of the two isthmian grants rather than the ratification of a treaty.[61] Through the influence of the Sloo grantees, the treaty was once rejected in the Senate.

There were many other impediments to the ratification of the treaty.   Senator Shields, of Illinois, bitterly fought the treaty because it gave American money to build up the power of Santa Anna, whom he designated as a heart-

---

[55] N. Y. *Times,* Jan. 20, 1854.

[56] *Cong. Globe,* 33 Cong., 1 sess. (1853–1854), XXVIII, pt. 1, p. 207. N. Y. *Herald,* Apr. 6, 1854.

[57] N. O. *Daily Picayune,* Feb. 10, 1854.

[58] N. Y. *Times,* Jan. 28, 1854.

[59] N. O. *Daily Picayune,* Feb. 10, 1854.

[60] N. Y. *Journal of Commerce,* Apr. 6, 1854.

[61] *Ibid.*

less, tyrannical, military despot.[62]  Houston, of Texas, opposed it because of his personal hostility to the negotiator of the treaty.[63]  He was absent from the Senate during the period of ratification, but was paired with friends of the treaty.[64]  Judah P. Benjamin was also absent during the same period, and his influence and vote were missed by the friends of the treaty.[65]  The disclosure in the Senate of the connection of Ward with the treaty was a severe blow to ratification.[66]  On straight party lines the Democrats also lacked a two-thirds majority in the Senate, as that body was composed of thirty-seven Democrats, twenty-one Whigs, and two Free-Soilers.[67]

Action upon the treaty began on March 13, when it was read for the second time and considered by the Senate as in the Committee of the Whole.[68]  On March 15 it was again considered.  On that date Mason advocated confirmation by the Senate, while Gwin opposed ratification unless the treaty should be essentially amended.[69]

Lines of cleavage began at once to appear in the discussions and votes in the Senate.  In addition to the antislavery irreconcilables, four other distinct groups were formed in the Senate.  A group of senators led by Senator Mason advocated ratification of the treaty in its original form.  They favored an indemnity for the Garay grantees, but were opposed to any recognition of the Sloo grant. Allen, of Rhode Island, Hunter, of Virginia, Adams, of Mississippi, and Dodge, of Wisconsin, were members of

[62] N. O. *Daily Picayune*, Mar. 29, 1854.

[63] Texas *State Gazette*, May 27, 1854.

[64] Phila. *North American*, Mar. 18, 1854.

[65] *Ibid.*

[66] N. Y. *Times*, Apr. 7, 1854.

[67] *Cong. Globe*, 33 Cong., 1 sess. (1853–1854), XXVIII, pt. 1, p. 1.

[68] *S. Ex. Journal*, IX, 264.

[69] Charleston *Daily Courier*, Mar. 20, 1854.

this bloc. The California senators demanded a larger acquisition of Mexican territory and a port on the Gulf of California. Gwin and Weller, with the aid of Shields, of Illinois, made this a *sine qua non* to the ratification of the treaty. The senators who favored a southern transcontinental railroad were led by Rusk, of Texas, the most aggressive supporter of the treaty. This group demanded only a boundary line that secured an eligible route for a southern railroad. Another bloc was composed of senators who demanded the recognition of the Sloo grant by the government. Bell, of Tennessee, was the leader, with Bayard, of Delaware, James, of Rhode Island, and Geyer, of Missouri, as assistants. Thus, the situation in the Senate resembled that of 1850 when the compromise measures were discussed, and the Gadsden treaty received the same treatment as was given to the Omnibus Bill.

General debate on the treaty continued from March 15 to March 27. The Senate called upon the President to furnish various documents, such as the instructions of Gadsden,[70] the amount of the claims of the United States and Mexico under the treaty,[71] and the correspondence in regard to the isthmian grants.[72] The Sloo group insisted upon the recognition by the government of the Sloo grant. On February 13, the Senate, on the motion of Bell, called upon the President to furnish a copy of the Conkling convention.[73] On March 13, Bell offered an amendment to the Gadsden treaty for the recognition of the Sloo grant, but the amendment was rejected by the Committee on Foreign Relations.[74] On March 14, President Pierce sent a copy of the Conkling convention to

[70] *S. Ex. Journal*, IX, 266.
[71] *Ibid.*, 268.
[72] *Ibid.*, 240.
[73] *Ibid.*
[74] *Ibid.*, 264–266.

Senate, for the purpose of information but not for ratification.[75]  He opposed the convention because (1) it assumed that the Garay claim was invalid; (2) it bound the United States to guarantee the contract of a private company with Mexico; (3) the obligations assumed by the United States were for a long duration of time; (4) the convention with Great Britain of April 19, 1850, included any interoceanic connection by the Isthmus of Tehuantepec.

On March 27, the intrigue of Ward was discovered by the Senate.  A letter of Ward to one of the Mexican commissioners was read by a senator, which at once caused the Senate to demand of the President all the correspondence between Ward and Gadsden relative to the negotiation of the treaty.[76]  On April 1, President Pierce sent the correspondence to the Senate, accompanied by a message in which he denied that the unofficial correspondence of Ward conveyed his correct views or wishes.  He declared that Ward had received no instructions to include the Garay or Sloo grants in the proposed treaty.  Although President Pierce regretted that Ward had departed from his instructions and had failed to give Gadsden the correct information, he imputed to him no design of misrepresentation.[77]

The discovery of the intrigues of Ward had a very unfavorable effect upon the ratification of the treaty.  The refusal of the Senate to print the correspondence of Ward caused the New York *Herald* to declare that it was so barefaced that the Senate, from a sense of shame and self-respect, feared to print it, lest it might reach the newspapers.[78]  Senators were said to be disgusted with the indirect and

[75] *Ibid.*, 265–266.
[76] *Ibid.*, 271.  Phila. *North American*, Apr. 1, 1854.
[77] *S. Ex. Journal*, IX, 276.
[78] N. Y. *Herald*, Apr. 6, 1854.

irregular mode of diplomatic procedure.[79]    Moreover, the
disclosure further excited northern prejudices against the
treaty.[80]    The friends of General Gadsden both within
and outside the Senate, began to place the blame of the
affair upon Ward.[81]    The New York *Tribune* published
an article on the "Secret History of the Gadsden Treaty"
which explained how Gadsden had been deceived by
Ward.[82]    In a long letter which was mainly a defense of
the Garay grant, Ward replied to these charges.  He
denied that General Gadsden had been misled by him,
through the means of any "professed instructions or
otherwise." [83]

The effect of this disclosure was soon shown by the votes
in the Senate.    The advocates of the treaty were unable to
muster more than a margin of a few votes.    Article I,
which defined the boundary line, was struck out by a vote
of 19 to 17, but the motion of Shields that the line be
moved farther south, in order to get a port on the Gulf of
California, was defeated by a vote of 21 to 20.[84]    Both the
Mason and the Rusk factions opposed this motion.    On
April 5, Gwin offered a resolution that the boundary line
be extended to the thirty-first parallel of north latitude,
which would include the northern part of the state of
Sonora and his desired port on the Gulf of California.
This resolution was defeated by a vote of 12 to 26.[85]    On
April 6, a motion to lay the treaty on the table lacked only
two votes of passage.[86]    Mason then retired, and his place

[79] N. Y. *Journal of Commerce*, Apr. 7, 1854.
[80] N. Y. *Times*, Apr. 7, 1854.
[81] N. Y. *Herald*, Apr. 12, 1854.
[82] N. Y. *Tribune*, Apr. 13, 1854.
[83] *Ibid.*, Apr. 17, 1854.
[84] *S. Ex. Journal*, IX, 278.
[85] *Ibid.*, 280.
[86] *Ibid.*, 282.

as the leader for ratification of the treaty was taken by Rusk.[87]  In regard to these proceedings in the Senate, the New York *Times* declared that "the treaty, there is little doubt, is essentially used up. It has been made the combination of adverse conditions . . . the disclosures being the most effective agent to this end." [88]

Under the leadership of Rusk, efforts were made to revive the treaty. All that Rusk desired from the treaty was enough Mexican territory for a southern railroad route to the Pacific. He sided with the members of the Sloo group in order to secure their votes for the ratification of the treaty. In order to reconcile the northern anti-slavery senators to the treaty, the acquisition of any large amount of Mexican territory was opposed. On April 10, Rusk offered a new boundary line between the two countries, which gave to the United States only enough Mexican territory for a railroad route. This amendment was accepted by a vote of 32 to 14.[89]  Another attempt of Gwin to secure a large cession of Mexican territory was defeated by a vote of 18 to 26.[90]  The reduction of the amount of territory was praised by the Charleston *Daily Courier,* because it secured a railroad route, and by the reduction, the votes of the northern senators were obtained for ratification of the treaty.[91]

On April 12, Rusk continued to alter the treaty in order to render it acceptable to all groups. [Article II, which released the United States from article XI of the treaty of Guadalupe Hidalgo, was rejected because it promised to aid Mexico against the American Indians.[92]] The new

---

[87] N. Y. *Times,* Apr. 6, 1854.
[88] *Ibid.,* Apr. 7, 1854.
[89] *S. Ex. Journal,* IX, 284.
[90] *Ibid.*
[91] Charleston *Daily Courier,* Apr. 17, 1854.
[92] *S. Ex. Journal,* IX, 290.

article inserted by Rusk simply declared article XI to be abrogated. The motion of Rusk to reject articles III and IV, by which the United States agreed to pay Mexico $15,-000,000 and American claimants against Mexico $5,000,000, was accepted by a unanimous vote.[93] His substitute for these articles, which reduced the sum payable to Mexico to $7,000,000 and made no mention of private claims, was agreed to by a vote of 30 to 13.[94] On the motion of Gwin, article VIII, which promised the mutual coöperation of both countries in suppressing filibustering expeditions was rejected.[95]

These amendments caused the Charleston *Daily Courier* to change from its former tone of praise. The Washington correspondent reported that "it cannot be expected that the President will adopt the Senate substitute."[96] It was charged that the northern senators agreed to lower Santa Anna's compensation more than half so that the treaty would be unacceptable to him. On April 17, the amendment of Bell in favor of the Sloo grant came to a vote. Although President Pierce had refused to submit the Conkling convention to the Senate and the Committee on Foreign Relations had rejected Bell's amendment, this did not stop the activity of the friends of the Sloo grant. Bell, on April 17, offered in the Committee of the Whole a new article to the treaty, under which the Sloo grant was recognized by both governments, and the company formed under the grant was promised governmental protection. The United States was given the right "to extend its protection as it shall judge wise to the Company . . . when it may feel sanctioned and warranted by the public or

---

[93] *Ibid.*, 292.
[94] *Ibid.*
[95] *Ibid.*, 293.
[96] Charleston *Daily Courier*, Apr. 17, 1854.

international law.'' [97]   This amendment was defeated by only four votes. Rusk favored it, while Mason and his followers voted for its rejection.

As no other amendments were offered in the Committee of the Whole, the treaty, on April 17, was reported to the Senate. After the alterations of the committee had been accepted, Bell again offered his Sloo amendment as a new article in the treaty.[98]  By a vote of 28 to 18 it was again rejected, although it lacked only two votes of the two-thirds majority necessary for its acceptance.

Immediately after the rejection of Bell's amendment, the vote on ratification was taken and the treaty was defeated by a vote of 27 to 18.[99]  Three more votes in the affirmative would have ratified the treaty.  Twelve of the eighteen negative votes were cast by anti-slavery senators of the North.  Bell voted for ratification, but three Sloo men, Bayard, Geyer, and James, refused to accept the treaty without the Sloo amendment.  The action of Mason and friends of the Garay grant in voting against the Bell amendment, influenced the friends of the Sloo grant to vote against the treaty.[100]  Gwin and Shields refused to vote for the treaty unless it included a large acquisition of Mexican territory and a port on the Gulf of California. Butler, of South Carolina, was the only southern senator to vote against the ratification of the treaty.  The defeat of the treaty was therefore due to a combination of northern irreconcilables, friends of the Sloo grant, and the California group.  The Senate had been unable either to ratify the original treaty sent by the President or to accept a substitute framed by its own body.

[97] *S. Ex. Journal,* IX, 299.
[98] *Ibid.,* 302.
[99] *Ibid.,* 306.
[100] N. Y. *Times,* Apr. 18, 1854.

Rejection of the treaty brought forth both adverse and favorable comments from the press. The Washington *Union* was disappointed over the repudiation of the treaty.[101] The Richmond *Enquirer* considered the rejection of the treaty, "whatever its defects, to be a calamity to the country." [102]   In Texas the defeat was regarded as "more disastrous to the interests and progress of the South, and especially our own State, than any event in our congressional history of the past century—striking a blow at the success of the southern route for a Pacific railroad." [103]   The Washington *Star* declared that the unconstitutional action of eighteen senators would soon lead to a war, and the consequent acquisition of Mexico by the United States as a means of indemnity.[104]

Favorable comments on the rejection of the treaty came from both northern and southern newspapers. The Charleston *Daily Courier* reminded its readers that it was not the Gadsden treaty that had been rejected, but an emasculated project framed by the Senate and unacceptable to either President Pierce or Santa Anna.[105]   The Cincinnati *Daily Enquirer* declared that the action of the Senate would meet with the approval of the country, as it was folly to pay a large sum of money for barren land "which is certain to become ours in a few years at any rate." [106]   The Philadelphia *Public Ledger* thought that the Southern Pacific railroad would have a doubtful future, as the bonus for that railroad, the Gadsden treaty, was now defeated.[107]   The New York *Herald* was especially jubilant over the action of the Senate.

[101] Washington *Union*, Apr. 19, 1854.
[102] Richmond *Enquirer*, Apr. 19, 1854.
[103] Texas *State Gazette*, May 6, 1854.
[104] From Savannah *Daily Republican*, Apr. 22, 1854.
[105] Charleston *Daily Courier*, Apr. 22, 1854.
[106] Cincinnati *Daily Enquirer*, Apr. 21, 1854.
[107] Phila. *Public Ledger*, Apr. 19, 1854.

The assertion of the Charleston *Daily Courier* that the real treaty was not dead proved to be true. There were forces and influences at work which made impossible the final rejection of the treaty. The administration now took a firm stand in the matter. In regard to the treaty as amended by the Senate, President Pierce declared that he would reject it with contempt.[108] He also let it be known that if the Gadsden treaty were not ratified, the responsibility of a war would rest upon the Senate.[109] It was rumored in the newspapers that Santa Anna would not hazard his power by the acceptance of any reduction in his compensation, nor make a new treaty after the rejection of the Gadsden treaty.[110]

In the meantime, during the discussion of the treaty in the Senate, the Southern and Western Commercial Convention was held at Charleston, South Carolina, April 8–15, 1854, of which, Senator Dawson, of Georgia, was the chairman. The Gadsden treaty and a railroad route through northern Mexico were important topics of discussion in the convention. Combs, of Kentucky, was pleased that a treaty had been made with Mexico which gave the South a suitable railroad route.[111] Gadsden attended the convention and on April 14, made an address.[112] In this speech he said that his first instructions were to settle all the difficulties which had arisen between the two countries over the enforcement of the treaty of Guadalupe Hidalgo. Prominent among these, he asserted, was the boundary dispute which involved the railroad route. He charged that Bartlett had been

---

[108] Charleston *Daily Courier*, Apr. 22, 1854.

[109] *Ibid.*

[110] *Ibid.*, Apr. 24, 1854.

[111] *De Bow's Review*, Aug. 1854 (XVII, 207).

[112] *Ibid.*, Oct. 1854 (XVII, 408).
Charleston *Daily Courier*, Apr. 28, 1854.

appointed at the instance of Governor Seward, of New York, and that his surrender of the Mesilla valley was in accordance with the instructions of Seward to exclude the South from the railroad route secured by the treaty. He further declared that the new treaty recovered the territory which had been surrendered by Bartlett, as the new boundary line had been determined and arranged in order to secure a railroad route to the Pacific.[113]

After the customary display of oratory, banquets, and toasts, the Committee on Resolutions, with Pike, of Arkansas, as chairman, reported on April 14 a series of resolutions. A resolution was adopted by the convention which declared that the "southern road ought to connect at suitable points on the Mississippi between New Orleans and St. Louis, centering at some point in Texas, or near the thirty-second degree of north latitude to the Rio Grande and western border of Texas, by the route designated in her law to charter the Mississippi, El Paso and Pacific railroad and thence to the Gulf of California." [114]

Upon the adoption of this resolution, the Committee on Resolutions proposed another, which declared that, "in the deliberate judgment of the convention the Gadsden treaty with the government of Mexico, as published in the newspapers ought to be ratified by the Senate of the United States, at least so far as it had seemed the best route for the purpose of a southern railroad from the western limits of Texas to the Pacific." [115] This resolution caused a general discussion of the Gadsden treaty. Polk, of Tennessee, was certain that every northern member in Congress was opposed to the treaty because it furnished the

[113] *De Bow's Review*, Oct. 1854 (XVII, 408).

N. Y. *Herald*, Apr. 19, 1854.

[114] N. Y. *Herald*, Apr. 19, 1854. This paper had a special reporter at the convention.

[115] *Ibid.*

only practicable southern route for the Pacific railroad.[116]
Gadsden also entered the discussion, and declared that
he, as a member of the convention, would not favor such
a resolution, as "the treaty might contain many propositions which were unknown to the delegates and which if
known they might not approve." [117]   He assured the convention that President Pierce would do all that should be
done.   Jones, of Tennessee, although he pledged his aid
to the southern road was not in favor of meddling with
an uncertain subject.[118]   Dawson, as chairman of the convention, expressed the opinion that there was no need of
precipitation in the matter.[119]   He believed that the
southern senators would look after the interests of the
South.   The resolution was then withdrawn by the chairman of the Committee on Resolutions.

True to the prediction of Dawson that the southern
senators would secure the ratification of the treaty, the
senators at the convention, Dawson, of Georgia, Jones, of
Tennessee, and Clay, of Alabama returned to Washington
and began to work zealously for the passage of the treaty.
In this effort they were aided by the Sloo group.   On
April 18, on the motion of James, of Rhode Island, a
stanch Sloo man, the rejected treaty was reconsidered.[120]

Under the leadership of Dawson and Jones, the treaty
was forced through the Senate.   The only real opposition
to ratification came from the northern anti-slavery group.
Upon the motion of Mason, the boundary line was slightly
altered so that it ran a little south of the line previously
designated by the Senate.[121]   Only eleven senators opposed

---

[116] *Ibid.*
[117] *Ibid.*
[118] *De Bow's Review,* Oct. 1854 (XVII, 410).
[119] *Ibid.*
[120] *S. Ex. Journal,* IX, 306.
[121] *Ibid.,* 309.

this change. The amount of compensation to Mexico was increased from $7,000,000 to $10,000,000.[122] The amendment of Bell, which promised protection to the work of the Sloo company on the part of both the United States and Mexico, was accepted by a vote of 30 to 14.[123] Dawson, Clay, Jones, and Rusk voted for it, while the Mason group continued to oppose it.

On April 25, the treaty was ratified by a vote of 33 to 12.[124] With the exception of Dodge, of Iowa, and Shields, of Illinois, the opposition to ratification was composed of the anti-Nebraska and anti-slavery senators of the North. Gwin was absent when the final vote was taken. Eleven northern Democrats and one Whig voted with the southern Democrats and Whigs for the ratification of the treaty.

Thus a shadow of the treaty negotiated by Gadsden was ratified by the Senate. The territory acquired by the original treaty was reduced nine thousand square miles by the Senate.[125] Article XI was declared to be abrogated without any promise to Mexico of future protection from the American Indians. No mention was made of the prior claims of Mexico under this article. There was also no mention of private claims in the treaty in its final form. The sum paid to Mexico was reduced $5,000,000 and the American government refused to coöperate with Mexico in the suppression of filibustering expeditions. Territory for a railroad route had been acquired, but no natural boundary, nor a port on the Gulf of California was secured. Furthermore, an article was inserted into the treaty by the Senate, which gave the United States the right to intervene in Mexico to protect the work of the

[122] *Ibid.*, 310.
[123] *Ibid.*, 311.
[124] *Ibid.*
[125] *U. S. and Mexican Claims Commission, 1868*, Pub. of Dept. of State, III, 38.

Sloo grantees, whenever the government considered it necessary. To secure the ratification of the treaty, its friends were compelled to accept this article. The Sloo people could proudly boast, as they did, that they had "carried the treaty through the Senate."[126]

The same outside tactics that were used when the treaty was negotiated were conspicuous during the period of ratification. Gadsden declared that the long period of time, from the negotiation of the treaty to the action of the Senate, gave opportunity for the Sloo and Hargous companies to set intrigues on foot.[127] An exciting battle was waged between the Garay and Sloo men during the proceedings of the senate in regard to the treaty. For the Garay people it was simply a change of venue, as L. E. and L. S. Hargous returned to America from Mexico on the same boat with Gadsden.[128] The New York *Tribune* declared that the Garay men fought most desperately, and that "they were not lacking in the sinews of war—filthy lucre."[129] W. H. Aspinwall, of the Pacific Mail Steamship Company, opposed the treaty because he did not wish his claims against Mexico to be decided by a tribunal, as was designated in the treaty.[130] Speculators in the United States who held Mexican Indian claims, opposed the ratification of the treaty. Senator Sumner presented in the Senate a remonstrance to that effect.[131] The newspapers were full of charges and countercharges as to the speculation connected with the ratification of the treaty.

With all due allowance for the mistakes of the press, the ratification of the treaty offered a gala day for speculators

[126] Charleston *Daily Courier*, May 1, 1854.

[127] Doyle to Clarendon, July 3, 1854, F. O., Mex., vol. 268, no. 71.

[128] N. O. *Daily Picayune*, Jan. 13, 1854.

[129] N. Y. *Tribune*, May 2, 1854.

[130] Aspinwall to Marcy, Feb. 15, 1854, Marcy Papers, vol. 48.

[131] N. Y. *Times*, Feb. 1, 1854.

and lobbyists. The Richmond *Enquirer* announced that "the swarm of speculators around the treaty had given it a bad name." [132] The New Orleans *Daily Delta* declared that the opposition to the Gadsden treaty had developed in a striking degree some of the worst features of congressional legislation, such as lobbyism and sectionalism, and that peculiar interests of individuals and classes were arrayed with great effect against a measure of the highest natural advantage and importance.[133] Marcy in a communication to Cripps, Secretary of the American legation in Mexico, admitted that there had been much outdoor opposition to the treaty in Washington and feared that the same influences would attempt to have the treaty rejected by the Mexican government.[134] Gadsden in 1856 urged Secretary Campbell to submit immediately to the Senate his Postal convention with Mexico in order that it might be confirmed before outsiders could combine to defeat it, as they had defeated a treaty on a former occasion.[135]

Thus, the sectionalism that was shown in the debates on the transcontinental railroad during the previous session of Congress was complicated by other issues in the ratification of the Gadsden treaty. Some southern senators considered the recognition of the Garay or the Sloo grant of more importance than the acquisition of a railroad route or an extension of southern territory. Likewise, some northern senators, who opposed a southern railroad to the Pacific and the expansion of slave territory, voted for the treaty because they were interested in these Mexican concessions. Sectional tendencies were present, however, in the form of opposition to a southern railroad to the Pacific

---

[132] Richmond *Enquirer*, Apr. 10, 1854.

[133] From N. Y. *Journal of Commerce*, May 12, 1854.

[134] Marcy to Cripps, May 6, 1854, Dept. of State, Inst., Mex., vol. 17, no. 25.

[135] Gadsden to Buchanan, Aug. 2, 1856, Buchanan Papers.

and the extension of slave territory. The final vote on the treaty was sectional, in the sense that the majority of the negative votes were cast by the northern anti-slavery senators. This group, with Seward as the leader, determined to hinder both the acquisition of slave territory and the construction of a transcontinental railroad through the southern states.[136] Seward introduced in the Senate, on December 27, 1853, a bill for a Pacific railroad, to be built on a route north of the fortieth parallel of north latitude.[137] The New York *Journal of Commerce* somewhat ineloquently declared that the treaty was opposed by such men as Sumner, Seward, and Chase, upon the narrow ground that the treaty added a strip of territory to the "southern end of the liver." [138] Gadsden asserted that, between private speculation on one side and sectional prejudices on the other, the treaty had been emasculated.[139] So strong was this northern opposition to further acquisition of southern or slave territory that Rusk reduced the amount of territory to be acquired, with the hope of winning northern votes for the treaty.

The uncertainty as to the relative parts sectionalism and speculation played in the ratification of the treaty could be eliminated, if the injunction of secrecy had been removed from the proceedings of the Senate. As soon as the treaty had been ratified, the press demanded the publication of the proceedings of the Senate. The New York *Tribune* desired this publicity because it concerned the honor of the Senate and the reputation of the President, the Secretary

---

[136] N. Y. *Journal of Commerce*, Apr. 7, 1854.

[137] *Cong. Globe*, 33 Cong., 1 sess. (1853–54), XXVI, pt. 1, p. 97. *Daily Indiana State Sentinel*, Jan. 7, 1854.

[138] N. Y. *Journal of Commerce*, Mar. 22, 1854.

[139] Gadsden to a friend, in N. Y. *Journal of Commerce*, Aug. 17, 1854.

of State, and General Gadsden.[140]   Another paper desired
the removal of secrecy so that it might be shown how Gadsden had been made the tool of "mean, low and contemptible
men." [141]   The Albany *Argus* demanded that the people
should see how their servants had acted in this matter.   It
was also considered especially important that the House of
Representatives should have these facts, before that body
voted to establish a new vice regency of Spain on the
southern border of the United States.[142]   The Detroit *Free
Press,* however, opposed the removal of the injunction of
secrecy from the proceedings.   It declared that "it certainly would be a vulgar and most undignified proceeding
to publish these virulent attacks on Santa Anna, to be
sent out to Mexico at the same time with a treaty." [143]

All attempts in the Senate to remove the injunction of
secrecy failed.   On April 26, the motion of Shields to this
effect failed by a vote of 13 to 26.[144]   Again, on June 29,
Shields attempted to have the injunction removed, where-
upon the matter was referred to the Committee on Foreign
Relations but no action was taken by that body.[145]   The
energy of Shields in this matter attracted attention.   The
New York *Times* attributed his efforts to a desire to get his
speech, in which he had abused Santa Anna, before the
public.[146]

It was with much reluctance that President Pierce agreed
to the altered treaty which was ratified by the Senate.   He
was annoyed at the manner in which his wishes with

[140] N. Y. *Tribune,* Apr. 20, 1854.
[141] Augusta *Daily Chronicle and Sentinel,* May 2, 1854.
[142] Albany *Argus,* Apr. 27, 1854.
[143] Detroit *Free Press,* May 4, 1854.
[144] *S. Ex. Journal,* IX, 316.
[145] *Ibid.,* 342.
[146] N. Y. *Times,* Apr. 28, 1854.

respect to the treaty had been ignored.[147]   He had taken
the position that the government should not interfere to
protect private companies in foreign countries, and he was
therefore, bitterly opposed to the Sloo amendment.[148]   This
article also contained the principles of the Conkling convention which he had refused to submit to the Senate for
ratification.   At one time, he had almost decided to drop
the treaty and to begin new negotiations with Mexico and
only the earnest entreaties of certain senators, especially
Senator Rusk, caused him to accept the amendments.[149]
Secretary Marcy informed Gadsden that the President had
determined to ratify the treaty only because of the magni-
tude of the difficulties with Mexico, and because the treaty
removed those of the most threatening character.[150]   In
consideration of the amendments to the treaty, it was
decided that the Mexican minister at Washington lacked
the power to ratify it.   It was therefore sent back to Mexico
through a special messenger of the Mexican legation, un-
ratified by President Pierce, but with the assurance of ratification if Santa Anna should agree to the amendments.[151]

The scene of the battle for the ratification of the treaty
was, therefore, changed from Washington to Mexico City.
Gadsden was ordered to return to Mexico.   In the meantime, Secretary Marcy instructed Cripps, *chargé d'affaires
ad interim* to urge upon Santa Anna the acceptance of the
treaty.[152]   Cripps was advised to use haste in the matter,
so as to counteract the outside influences hostile to the

[147] Doyle to Clarendon, July 3, 1854, F. O., Mex., vol. 268, no. 71.
[148] Charleston *Daily Courier*, May 1, 1854.
[149] *Ibid.*, May 10, 1854.
[150] Marcy to Gadsden, May 11, 1854, Dept. of State, Inst., Mex.,
vol. 17, no. 27.
[151] Doyle to Clarendon, July 3, 1854, F. O., Mex., vol. 268, no. 71.
[152] Marcy to Cripps, May 6, 1854, Dept. of State, Inst., Mex., vol.
17, no. 25.

treaty. He was to inform the Mexican government that it would have to accept the treaty in the present form, as any attempt to change it would result in its defeat by the United States Senate. Before the arrival of Gadsden in Mexico City, Cripps had several conferences with Santa Anna and Bonilla in which he urged them to accept and ratify the modified treaty.[153] In these conferences, Bonilla pointed out to Cripps the deficiencies of the treaty. He expressed his unqualified disapproval because it did not adjust the issues between the two nations so as to promise harmony of relations in the future. He objected to the treaty because the private claims on neither side were settled, and because the United States was given the right to protect a private interest and speculation, on conditions which involved the "surrender of nationality in the right of eminent domain."

The insertion of the Sloo amendment by the Senate caused the British minister, Doyle, to oppose the ratification of the treaty by the Mexican government. He feared that this article would be prejudicial to the British isthmian plans. Before the arrival of Gadsden in Mexico, Doyle had advised Santa Anna not to allow the United States to secure a foothold in the interior of the country, nor to grant any special privilege to that nation which would infringe upon the Mexican treaties with other countries.[154] He urged Santa Anna either to reject the treaty or to include an article which would allow American intervention only at the request of the Mexican government.[155]

Santa Anna listened gladly to the arguments of Doyle.

[153] Gadsden to Marcy, June 9, 1854, Dept. of State, Des., Mex., vol. 18, no. 31.
[154] Doyle to Clarendon, June 2, 1854, F. O., Mex., vol. 267, no. 69.
[155] *Ibid.* to *ibid.*, July 3, 1854, *ibid.*, vol. 268, no. 71.

He informed the latter that he would reject the treaty if Doyle would authorize the suspension of the Mexican payment of British claims and use his influence with the ministers of France and Spain to the same end. Such an act, Doyle replied, he had no power to authorize.[156] Doyle was more excited over the American aggression than was the British Foreign Office. Clarendon demanded only the neutralization of the isthmian route. He considered that article VIII of the Clayton-Bulwer treaty protected British interests in the Isthmus of Tehuantepec.[157]

Gadsden was disgusted with the manner in which the Senate had altered his treaty. He returned to Mexico with the hope that the treaty would be rejected by Santa Anna. He was especially indignant that article III, which provided for the payment of private claims against Mexico, was eliminated. The claimants, he assured Marcy, would seriously embarrass the legation and continue the issues with Mexico.[158] He advised Marcy to break off negotiations with Santa Anna and to treat with the party which was certain to supersede him, and whose need would be as great as Santa Anna's.[159] He informed Marcy that he felt deprived of both the will and the ability to urge any considerations in favor of a treaty of assumed agreement, so unequal and repugnant to one party.[160] In a weak letter to Bonilla, he urged the acceptance of the amended treaty, upon the ground that it removed the most serious difficulties between the two

[156] *Ibid.*

[157] Clarendon to Doyle, Sept. 29, 1854; Oct. 31, 1854, *ibid.*, vol. 265, nos. 90, 99.

[158] Gadsden to Marcy, May 21, 1854, Dept. of State, Des., Mex., vol. 18.

[159] *Ibid.*

[160] *Ibid.* to *ibid.*, June 9, 1854, *ibid.*, vol. 18, no. 31.

countries and because there was no reason to hope that a different treaty would receive the approval of the United States Senate.[161]

Santa Anna, although he desired to reject the treaty, was in no position to do so. He was in great need of money and he needed it immediately. In the state of Guerrero a revolution was in progress which meant the overthrow of Santa Anna unless he could secure money enough to equip an army. The situation was so critical that Pickett, the American consul at Vera Cruz, informed Marcy that only the immediate ratification of the treaty could sustain Santa Anna for even a brief period.[162] There was also no certainty as to what attitude the United States government might take if the treaty was rejected. Almonte informed Santa Anna that rejection would in all probability mean war.[163]

Under these critical conditions, Santa Anna was forced to ratify the treaty. Doyle, after an unsuccessful interview with Santa Anna, informed Clarendon that Santa Anna and his ministers would sign anything that would secure ready money with which to prevent a revolution and their downfall.[164] As the treaty provided for its ratification within six months after the negotiation, no time was to be lost. Santa Anna therefore agreed to the treaty, and a special messenger, Senor Rafael, was sent to Almonte on June 7, with instructions to ratify the treaty.[165] Santa Anna declared later in life that he had accepted the amended treaty because he "recognized that it was im-

[161] Gadsden to Bonilla, June 6, 1854, *ibid.*, vol. 18, with no. 31.
[162] Pickett to Marcy, Apr. 7, 1854, Dept. of State, Cons. Let., Vera Cruz, vol. 6.
[163] Doyle to Clarendon, July 3, 1854, F. O., Mex., vol. 268, no. 71.
[164] *Ibid.*
[165] Gadsden to Marcy, June 17, 1854, Dept. of State, Des., Mex., vol. 18, no. 32.

politic to refuse their (the United States') consent, there remaining the satisfaction of having obtained for a piece of wild country, relatively what they gave for half of the national property." [166]   He considered it a great treaty compared with the ignominious treaty of Guadalupe Hidalgo.[167]

On June 20, Santa Anna's note of acceptance reached President Pierce.   On the following day, June 21, he informed the House of Representatives that the Mexican government had accepted the amendments of the Senate. He asked that the money necessary for the fulfillment of the terms of the treaty be placed at his disposal.[168]   The message was referred to the Committee of Ways and Means, and the next day, Houston, Chairman of the Committee, presented a bill to enable the President to fulfill the terms of the third article of the treaty with Mexico.[169]

The opponents of the treaty in Congress had not been idle since its ratification by the Senate.   Thomas H. Benton, an ardent opponent of the southern railroad route, early announced his plan to oppose the treaty when it came to the House of Representatives.   In a letter to the New York *Evening Post,* he declared that he would oppose it because it involved the privileges of the House of Representatives and because of its peculiar mode of negotiation.[170] Although he did not claim any particular knowledge as to its negotiation, the common rumor, he thought, was enough to require an investigation.   In a speech in the House of Representatives on May 19, he charged that the Kansas-

---

[166] *Documentos inéditas o muy raros para la historia de Méjico,* 2, 3.

[167] *Manifesto del Presidente de la república a la nacion,* 1855.

[168] *Cong. Globe,* 33 Cong., 1 sess. (1853–1854), XXVIII, pt. 2, p. 1466.

[169] *Ibid.,* 1476.

[170] From N. Y. *Tribune,* May 5, 1854.

Nebraska bill, the Gadsden treaty, and the Soulé mission were conceived at the same time and were parts of a grand movement of the slavocracy.[171]  The Gadsden treaty, he declared, was only another scheme of the South to get territory and to convert free soil into slave soil.

Benton took advantage of the first possible occasion to oppose the appropriation bill.  When Houston reported his bill, Benton at once asked for the opportunity to plead "the privileges of the House, the constitution of the United States and the people of the United States" before an appropriation was made.[172]  On June 26, he delivered a strong speech against the appropriation of the money.[173] He began his argument with a declaration that the prerogatives of the House had been infringed upon, because the President had not transmitted with his message the correspondence connected with the negotiation of the treaty. He raised the old question which arose first in connection with the Jay treaty, as to whether the President and Senate could alone make and ratify a treaty which involved an appropriation, without the consent of the House of Representatives, and whether the latter body could block a treaty by its refusal to appropriate the money to enforce it. Benton presented five resolutions in which he showed how the privileges of the House had been overstepped.[174] According to his argument, unless the House of Representatives had the right to investigate, the purse of the American people would be at the mercy of "a secret presidential resolve, a secret senatorial vote, and a secret

[171] *Cong. Globe*, 33 Cong., 1 sess. (1853–1854), XXVIII, pt. 2, p. 1233.

[172] *Ibid.*, 1476.

[173] *Ibid.*, 1519.

[174] *Cong. Globe*, 33 Cong., 1 sess. (1853–1854), XXIX, App., p. 1036.

bargain with any foreign potentate, legitimate or illegitimate." [175]

Benton opposed the treaty, however, for reasons other than the preservation of the honor of the House of Representatives. The acquisition of Mexican territory by the treaty was an indirect blow at the central transcontinental railroad route, of which Benton was the great exponent. He soon left his original objection, and the greater part of his speech was a severe denunciation of the treaty because it secured a southern railroad route. Documents were produced by Benton to show that the government was paying $10,000,000 for the privilege of a railroad through Chihuahua and Sonora, which Robert J. Walker had secured for $6,500.[176] The country was described as "so utterly desolate, desert and God-forsaken that . . . a wolf could not make his living there." "In vain," Benton declared, "do we ask for a road, any kind of one . . . rail, wagon, horse trail or footpath upon our own territory. It is all refused while millions are lavished upon ocean routes, and the two foreign roads actually provided for by this treaty. . . . The one hundred million company and the Sloo company get a road a piece by this treaty, the people of the United States get none." [177]

This speech brought forth replies in which the sincerity and motives of Benton were questioned. Bayly, of Virginia, said that the "shoe pinched Benton," simply because the South secured a railroad route.[178] It was declared that Benton opposed the treaty, not because it violated the privileges of the House of Representatives but because it

[175] *Ibid.*
[176] *Ibid.*, 1034.
[177] *Ibid.*, 1035.
[178] *Ibid.*, 1045.

interfered with a ''bantling of his own.'' [179]   The New York *Journal of Commerce* wrote that ''the Great Missourian thinks too much of St. Louis and 'my son-in-law' and too little of the Republic and its interests.'' [180]

The speeches of Benton and Bayly are typical of those delivered in the House concerning the appropriation bill. Objections to the treaty ranged over a large field.  It was urged that the treaty was a political intrigue of the South and President Pierce.  The land ceded by Mexico was declared to be worthless; ''territory'' was the appropriate term to be used in reference to it.  It was asserted that the land was so covered with Mexican land grants, that not one acre would come into the public domain.  It was denounced as another Cuban scheme, and as simply a means to retain Santa Anna in power.  One member claimed that it violated the Monroe Doctrine.

The greatest objection to the appropriation, however, was the fact that the President had not transmitted the correspondence relative to the negotiation of the treaty.  Both parties and sections were agreed in this objection and upon this point was expended the greatest amount of debate. It was maintained that the members were compelled to vote on a matter of which they knew practically nothing.

The Democrats had a large majority in the House and were therefore able to overcome all opposition of the Whigs and Free-Soilers.  Consequently the appropriation bill was railroaded through the House.  All attempts of the opponents of the treaty to secure the desired information from the President failed.  The Democrats claimed that it was too late for such a move; that the President was out of the city, and that any attempt to obtain the correspondence would delay ratification of the treaty in the allotted time.

[179] *Ibid.*
[180] N. Y. *Journal of Commerce*, June 28, 1854.

The usual method of a supporter of the treaty was to agree with the argument that the privileges of the House had been infringed upon, but to state that this case was an exception. No resolution to demand the correspondence from the President ever came to a vote. All such attempts were blocked by motions to go into the Committee of the Whole, by the claim of an absence of a quorum, or by adjournment. As ratification was necessary before July 1, no time was wasted by the supporters of the treaty. On June 27, by a vote of 94–58, it was decided that debate should close on the next day.[181]

The opponents of the treaty fought the appropriation bill to the very end. Although debate on the bill was closed, Benton in order to speak again, moved an amendment that the appropriation should be lowered one dollar, and then spoke on the amendment.[182] Peckham, Democrat of New York, moved an amendment to Benton's amendment, that the bill should not take effect until two days after the correspondence had been transmitted to the House by the President.[183] This amendment was defeated, but Haven, Whig of New York, offered a similar amendment, which designated that the bill should not become effective until nine days after the correspondence had been furnished the House.[184] In his remarks he asserted that the tenacity with which the correspondence was held showed that something was wrong. He declared that the administration was afraid to show the papers.

All attempts to change the bill, however, resulted in failure. The final vote showed 105 members in favor of the

[181] *Cong. Globe*, 33 Cong., 1 sess. (1853–1854), XXVIII, pt. 2, p. 1536.
[182] *Ibid.*, 1564.
[183] *Ibid.*
[184] *Ibid.*

appropriation and 63 in opposition.[185]   The vote, except in the case of the New York delegation, divided along party lines and closely resembled the vote on the Kansas-Nebraska bill.   In the affirmative were 40 northern Democrats, 49 southern Democrats, and 9 southern Whigs.   In opposition to the bill were 13 northern Democrats, 38 northern Whigs, 5 southern Whigs, 5 Free-Soilers, and Benton.   The New York delegation contained 22 Democrats, 10 Whigs, and one Free-Soiler.   Of this number the division was 6 ayes, 17 nays, and 10 not voting.   Only six New York Democrats favored the bill.   Eight of the 13 northern Democrats who opposed the bill were from New York. This vote is explained by the internal strife within the Democratic party of New York at that time.

The treaty was ratified by the President on June 29, 1854. Ratifications were exchanged with the Mexican legation on June 30, and on the same day President Pierce proclaimed the Gadsden treaty to be the law of the land.[186]   On the next day Almonte called at the Treasury Department and received a draft of $7,000,000, the first installment under the treaty.[187]

[185] *Ibid.,* 1565.
[186] Malloy, *Treaties and Conventions,* I, 1107.
[187] Washington *Union,* July 1, 1854.

# CHAPTER VI

## THE AFTERMATH OF THE GADSDEN TREATY

The Gadsden treaty did not settle all the existing issues between the United States and Mexico. It relieved only a few of the outstanding difficulties, such as the dispute over the boundary line and the question of Indian depredations, and even in regard to these, diplomatic correspondence continued. The matters which were left unsolved by the original treaty, and the items rejected by the United States Senate, became the bases for continued controversy. While the primary concern of this work is with the negotiation and ratification of the Gadsden treaty, it is also necessary to trace the working out of the treaty in the diplomatic relations between the two nations. This demands a study of the remainder of Gadsden's mission to Mexico.

The great obstacles to a final settlement of all the issues between the two nations, following the Gadsden treaty, were the unsettled conditions in Mexico, and the intense hatred of Santa Anna for the United States, a feeling reciprocated by Gadsden for the Mexican government. Gadsden, also did not have the confidence of Secretary Marcy and his lengthy communications to the Department of State received scant recognition. The policy of the administration toward Mexico became one of neglect and disregard. The same speculators who had been so active during the negotiation and ratification of the treaty now attempted to thwart every official effort of Gadsden,

146

and further, demanded the removal of Gadsden as minister to Mexico. European influence hostile to the United States continued manifest in Mexico. All these factors served as barriers to a better friendship between the two nations.

The main issues which arose between the two countries, out of the treaty, were in connection with claims for damages on the part of both nations, a boundary dispute, the payment of the $10,000,000 by the United States to Mexico, filibustering expeditions and Indian depredations. New controversies arose over the treatment of American citizens resident in Mexico and the commercial policy of Santa Anna.

The Mexican War did not mitigate the hatred of the Mexican people for the United States; and the expedition of William Walker into Lower California, and the negotiation of the Gadsden treaty had increased this feeling in Mexico.[1] Three months after the negotiation of the treaty, Gadsden declared that, "if the two governments are not at war, then relations have never been in harmony since the recall of Santa Anna and the influence exerted over him by a premier, a bigoted Catholic of the Jesuit order. . . . The preamble of the treaty which received the signature of both was responded to in stifled insincerity and that which was substituted by the Senate and forced on them, has only added to the smothered fires of deep rooted animosity towards the United States."[2]

Santa Anna showed his hostility to the United States by attacks on American institutions and by official acts and discriminations against American citizens resident in Mexico. "The institutions and policy of the United States," wrote Gadsden, "is [sic] the theme of constant

[1] Gadsden to Marcy, Sept. 2, 1854, Dept. of State, Des., Mex., vol. 18, no. 38.

[2] *Ibid.* to *ibid.*, Oct. 2, 1854, *ibid.*, vol. 18, no. 44.

attack in the semi-official journals of the day." [3]  *El Universal*, once owned by the Secretary of Foreign Relations Bonilla, and supplied by him with most of its editorials, was most violent in assaulting the policy of the United States. On October 30, 1854, in an editorial on the relations between the two countries, it declared that a detailed history of the past, "would be a register of ignominy for our neighbours, whilst it would prove to the civilized world, the good faith and candor with which Mexico has behaved." [4]  Santa Anna's attitude was clearly expressed in a manifesto of December 17, 1854, in which he compared the United States, "in its organization and aggressive policy with the federation of associates and robbers under the lead of the barbarian Álvarez." [5]

The arbitrary decrees of Santa Anna were extended to the American citizens resident in Mexico. Orders against freedom of speech, for the surrender of arms, and a detailed system of passports for travel from one location to another, were made applicable to all foreigners in Mexico, and were enforced with tyrannical passion against American citizens on every trifling pretext.[6]  In view of this official hostility, Pickett, American consul at Vera Cruz, declared that the sincere friendship promised by article I of the treaty of 1831, "should read sincere hatred and then it could be considered as religiously observed by the officials of the Government of His Most Serene Highness." [7]

The autocratic Mexican government and the anti-

[3] *Ibid.* to *ibid.*, Oct. 16, 1854, *ibid.*, vol. 18, no. 46.

[4] *El Universal*, Oct. 30, 1854.

[5] Gadsden to Marcy, Apr. 17, 1855, Dept. of State, Des., Mex., vol. 19, no. 61.

Álvarez was the leader of the revolution against Santa Anna.

[6] *Ibid.* to *ibid.*, Aug. 1854, *ibid.*, vol. 18, unofficial; Pickett to Marcy, Aug. 7, 1854, Dept. of State, Cons. Let., Vera Cruz, vol. 6.

[7] Pickett to Marcy, June 25, 1854, Dept. of State, Cons. Let., Vera Cruz, vol. 6.

Americanism of Santa Anna were very distasteful to Gadsden and deeply resented by him. He considered Santa Anna a usurper and believed that his sole aim was to create in Mexico a national distrust of American institutions and to extend absolutism in government and Roman Catholicism in religion. Gadsden looked upon Bonilla as the power behind the throne, and the main figure in the propagation of anti-Americanism in Mexico. The attacks on the United States by Bonilla in *El Universal* called forth protests from Gadsden. An insult to his country was considered a personal insult by Gadsden, and the clandestine attacks by Bonilla, he declared invited retaliation. Soon Bonilla was asking for the recall of Gadsden on the ground that he was insulting in diplomatic relations, while the latter asserted that the correspondence of Bonilla had become so antagonistic and arrogant that instead of reconciling unpleasant issues, it only widened the breach between the two governments and threatened to drive them into an open conflict.[8]

An event occurred soon after Gadsden's return to Mexico, which gave him an opportunity to show his contempt for the government of Santa Anna. September 27, was declared a national holiday in commemoration of the last victory of the Mexicans over the Spanish. This victory had been achieved by Santa Anna and the holiday was designed by him in order to supersede the claim of Itúrbide as being the liberator of Mexico. A decree was issued by Bonilla for the illumination of all public and private houses on the night of the celebration, with a fine as a penalty for those who refused to comply.[9] As this decree applied to foreigners in Mexico, Gadsden issued a state-

[8] Gadsden to Marcy, May 18, 1855, Dept. of State, Des., Mex., vol. 19, no. 63.

[9] Copy of order of Sept. 20, 1854, with Black to Marcy, Oct. 18, 1854, Dept. of State, Cons. Let., Mexico City, vol. 10.

ment on September 22, in which he advised the American citizens not to comply with the command of Bonilla.[10] The celebration, he declared was only an appeal to the patriotism of the Mexican citizens and the honoring of a military triumph in a civil war. It did not, he asserted, become Americans to participate in an affair, which was offensive to one party in Mexico. On the night of the 27th, Gadsden refused to illuminate the legation, and the American citizens also declined to participate in the celebration.

This action on the part of Gadsden occasioned the demand for his recall by the Mexican government. In a lengthy note of October 3, to Almonte, Bonilla declared that the diplomatic correspondence of Gadsden had been extremely offensive, that although his notes during the negotiation of the treaty had been insulting to the whole Spanish race, his attitude since the ratification had become more violent and hostile. Gadsden was charged by Bonilla with disregarding the proper diplomatic channels by his address of notes directly to Santa Anna, and with the misrepresentation of the periodical *El Universal*. The note of Gadsden to his fellow countrymen of September 22, was denounced as an aid to sedition, as it was placing the authority of the American minister above the laws and police regulations of Mexico.[11]

Secretary Marcy agreed to investigate the matter. Gadsden was informed of the demand of Bonilla, and was asked to answer the charges presented against him. Upon the receipt of this information, Gadsden immediately suspended diplomatic relations with the Mexican government, which suspension, he informed Bonilla, would continue until the attitude of President Pierce was made known or

---

[10] *Ibid.*

[11] Copy of note, with Almonte to Marcy, Oct. 19, 1854, Dept. of State, Notes to Dept., Mex. Leg., vol. 7.

until the complaints were withdrawn.[12]  Bonilla refused
to consider this note of Gadsden, and much to the disgust
of the latter, he continued correspondence with the American legation, and a semblance of diplomatic relations was
maintained.

An animated correspondence took place between Gadsden and Marcy over the demand of the Mexican government.  Marcy held that the charges were unfounded, but
he severely criticized Gadsden for the suspension of diplomatic relations with Mexico.  Such an act, he declared
induced a very embarrassing state of affairs.[13]  On the
other hand, Gadsden reproached Marcy for making an investigation of the matter.  He was gratified at the angry
complaints of Bonilla, for they gave, he asserted the
strongest evidence of the fidelity and resolution with
which the legation had fulfilled its obligation, in the vin-
dication of American integrity and institutions and in the
shielding of American citizens from the rude and tyrannical power of Santa Anna.[14]

On May 14, 1855, a second demand was made by the
Mexican government for the removal of Gadsden.
Almonte declared that, ''it has now become impossible for
General Gadsden to continue any longer the representative
of the United States in Mexico without compromising the
harmony and good understanding between the two republics.''[15]  On June 20, 1855, for the third time, Almonte
asked for the recall of Gadsden, asserting that the latter's

[12] Gadsden to Bonilla, Jan. 27, 1855, Dept. of State, Des., Mex.,
vol. 19, with no. 56.

[13] Marcy to Gadsden, Oct. 22, 1855, Dept. of State, Inst., Mex.,
vol. 17, no. 54.

[14] Gadsden to Marcy, Apr. 17, 1855, Dept. of State, Des., Mex.,
vol. 19, no. 61.

[15] Almonte to Marcy, May 14, 1855, Dept. of State, Notes to
Dept., Mex. Leg., vol. 8.

animosity toward Mexico had become daily more evident since his recall had been demanded.[16] The administration however, on all three occasions, refused to comply with the demand of the Mexican government, but the strained relations between Gadsden and the Mexican officials, rendered nugatory all attempts at reconciliation of the issues between the two countries.

In Mexico the autocratic rule of Santa Anna caused the outbreak of another revolution. Santa Anna came to regard himself as the dictator of Mexico, and in a decree of December 16, 1853, he informed the nation that he would continue invested with all his present powers as long as he should judge it necessary for the maintenance of public order.[17] Oppressive decrees were issued; the Jesuits were reinstated, and thought and action were regulated by the bayonet. The government became so offensive, that Black, American consul at Mexico City, declared, ''There is no doubt generally speaking that it is the most unpopular government that has ever existed in this country since their independence, although nothing dare be said against it.''[18]

The Plan of Ayutla, framed in the pueblo of Ayutla, of the department of Guerrero, March 1, 1854, by a group of revolutionary chiefs, became the platform of a revolution, led by Juan Álvarez, against Santa Anna.[19] The Plan of Ayutla denounced Santa Anna as a destroyer of Mexican freedom, and as unfaithful to his pledge to preserve the integrity of the nation. It promised the establishment of a republican form of government, the removal

---

[16] *Ibid.* to *ibid.*, June 20, 1855, *ibid.*

[17] Copy of decree with Gadsden to Marcy, Dec. 16, 1853, Dept. of State, Des., Mex., vol. 18, no. 16.

[18] Black to Marcy, Aug. 3, 1854, Dept. of State, Cons. Let., Mexico City, vol. 10.

[19] *Collección de las leyes fundamentales*, 315–317.

of vexatious decrees, and protection to foreign commerce.
An attempt by Santa Anna in the spring of 1854, to crush
this movement proved unsuccessful and the revolution
spread from Guerrero to other parts of the republic.  In
1854, declarations were made in Tamaulipas, Nuevo León,
Coahuila and Chihuahua in favor of the Plan of Ayutla.
This revolution in Mexico was welcomed by Gadsden
because its platform and leaders stood for the democratic
principles of the United States.  Accordingly his dispatches to Secretary Marcy were filled with praise for the
revolutionists or Liberal party in Mexico.  In September,
1854, he declared that it was the duty of the United States
to sympathize with, and sustain the Liberal party, and the
administration was urged to send an army into Mexico
for that purpose.[20]  His intense hatred for Santa Anna
caused him to urge President Pierce to dissolve relations
with the latter.  Although it may be too strong to say, as
has been charged, that Gadsden made his legation a ren-
dezvous for the Liberals, yet he desired to aid in every
way the revolution in Mexico against the rule of Santa
Anna.

While Gadsden favored the Liberals in Mexico, the
European diplomats gave assistance to Santa Anna.
Doyle, the British minister and his successor, Lettsom,
continued to advise Bonilla in regard to American affairs.
The notes of Gadsden to Bonilla were transmitted to the
British legation for perusal.[21]  At the suggestion of Doyle,
Almonte was instructed by the Mexican government to act
on American affairs in concert with the English and
French ministers at Washington.[22]  This intimacy of the
European diplomats with Santa Anna was not overlooked

[20] Gadsden to Marcy, Sept. 5, 1854, Dept. of State, Des., Mex.,
vol. 18, no. 41.

[21] Doyle to Clarendon, Jan. 2, 1855, F. O., Mex., vol. 276, no. 1.

[22] *Ibid.* to *ibid.*, May 3, 1855, *ibid.*, vol. 277, no. 44.

by Gadsden.  All signs, Gadsden assured Marcy, pointed
to an attempt on the part of Europe to recolonize the
Americas.  To avert this danger he advised the administration to aid in the overthrow of Santa Anna, whose ambition was to secure an European alliance with Mexico
against the United States.[23]

The Gadsden treaty opened many loopholes for American speculators, and their activity in Mexico was another
obstacle to amicable relations between the two nations.
The reciprocal claims of both countries, including those
under article XI and the Garay grant, remained unsettled.
The large sum of money which the Mexican government
realized by the treaty, made Mexico a profitable field for
American bankers.  But, just as Gadsden had opposed
the schemes of Hargous and Ward during the negotiation
of the treaty, he now refused to sanction the plans of the
"Plundering Cliques," as he termed the American bankers
and speculators who were participating in the spoils of
Mexico.  As a result, these men began to attack Gadsden
and soon he was forced to admit that "every diplomatic
lever has been wrested from my hands by those vigilant
and cormorant bankers." [24]

In order to secure the removal of Gadsden as minister
to Mexico, Hargous and Ward reported to Marcy, that
Gadsden was *non compos mentis,* and that his actions and
habits were unbecoming to an American minister.  Marcy
upon receiving this information began a secret investigation of the personal conduct of Gadsden, which was discovered by the latter.  To Marcy he declared, "that a
Secretary of State . . . should so respect [insidious]
whispering and debasing insinuations as to make enquiries

---

[23] Gadsden to Marcy, Oct. 4, 1856, Dept. of State, Des., Mex.,
vol. 19, no. 97.

[24] *Ibid.* to *ibid.,* July 11, 1855, *ibid.,* vol. 19, unofficial.

as to their credibility is a matter of such astonishment and surprise that I cannot falter in giving expression to.'' [25]   The investigation, Gadsden asserted was a personal insult, and he offered his resignation to Marcy.[26] An apology on the part of Marcy, did not, as Gadsden informed him, fully reconcile the matter.[27]  Unfriendly relations between the minister and Secretary of State continued until the removal of Gadsden in 1856, and it had an adverse influence on the diplomatic relations of the two countries.

A diplomatic issue arose over the payment by the United States to Mexico of the remaining installment of $3,000,000 under the Gadsden treaty.   On June 30, 1854, $7,000,000 had been paid to the Mexican government but within three months, this sum had been wasted on officials, speculators, hired troops and celebrations.[28]   Santa Anna personally appropriated $700,000 to indemnify himself for the depredations of the American armies on his plantations during the Mexican War.[29]   Although the treaty stipulated that the $3,000,000 should not be paid until the boundary line was established, the great need of money forced the Mexican government to demand this sum in advance. ''Sedulous approaches'' to this end, as Gadsden characterized them, were soon made to the American legation.[30]

Gadsden refused even to present the matter to the Department of State, and as a result, the Mexican government secured the money through American bankers in Mexico.   Between December 19, 1854, and July 9, 1855,

[25] *Ibid.* to *ibid.*, Apr. 16, 1855, Marcy Papers, vol. 59.

[26] *Ibid.* to *ibid.*, Apr. 18, 1855, *ibid.*

[27] *Ibid.* to *ibid.*, June 19, 1855, *ibid.*, vol. 61.

[28] *Ibid.* to *ibid.*, Jan. 3, 1855, Dept. of State, Des., Mex., vol. 18, private.

[29] *Ibid.* to *ibid.*, July 3, 1855, *ibid.*, vol. 19, no. 66.

[30] *Ibid.* to *ibid.*, Feb. 5, 1855, *ibid.*, vol. 19, no. 55.

drafts were made by the Mexican government on the
Treasury of the United States in favor of Howland and
Aspinwall, and Hargous Brothers.[31]   The official records
state that the loan was made at a discount of five per cent,
but according to Lettsom, one loan of $650,000 was sold
for $256,000,[32] while Gadsden declared that some of the
drafts were purchased at fifty per cent and others at not
less than thirty per cent below par, and asserted that the
profits of the bankers in the transaction amounted to
$1,000,000.[33]

Opposition to the payment of these drafts arose immediately in both the United States and Mexico.   Lobach and
Schepelen, merchants of New York City, advised Marcy to
use the $3,000,000 for the [indemnification] of Americans
who held Mexican Indian claims.[34]   The New Orleans
*Daily Picayune* objected, because the withholding of the
funds would force Mexico to open her ports to American
produce.[35]   Gadsden was opposed to the payment because
the money would sustain Santa Anna and would commit
the United States in favor of an absolute rule in Mexico.[36]

With the payment of the $3,000,000 to Mexico, there
was also closely connected a boundary dispute.   It was not
until 1856 that the boundary line was located, and in the
meanwhile it was necessary that some governmental jurisdiction should be placed over the territory ceded by Mexico.   Accordingly, on November 16, 1854, General Gar-

[31] *S. Ex. Docs.* (821), 34 Cong., 1 & 2 sess., XII, no. 8.

[32] Lettsom to Clarendon, Aug. 2, 1855, F. O., Mex., vol. 279,
no. 46.

[33] Gadsden to Marcy, June 5, 1855, Dept. of State, Des., Mex.,
vol. 19, private.

[34] Lobach and Schepelen to Marcy, Mar. 9, 1855, Dept. of State,
Misc. Let.

[35] From N. Y. *Herald*, Jan. 1, 1855.

[36] Gadsden to Marcy, Dec. 18, 1854, Dept. of State, Des., Mex.,
vol. 18, no. 31.

land, on the order of Governor Meriwether of New Mexico, took formal possession for the United States of the Mesilla valley.[37] This action, caused an immediate protest from the Mexican government and it also gave grounds for the demand by Mexico of the $3,000,000. The *Diario Oficial* declared that now the United States would have to pay the $3,000,000, "unless the right of might be alleged." [38] Almonte demanded of Marcy the immediate removal of the troops from the territory or the payment of the $3,000,000 to Mexico.[39]

The administration refused to give serious attention to the matter. Secretary Davis considered the hoisting of the American flag only a harmless ceremony.[40] Marcy would not acquiesce in the Mexican demands for satisfaction and although Almonte continued his protests, no action was taken by the American government, on either the boundary question or the payment of the $3,000,000 until the boundary line was established in 1856.

The claims left unsettled by the Gadsden treaty furnished the cause for another diplomatic controversy between the two nations. The majority of the American claims against Mexico consisted of illegal arrests and imprisonments, abrogation of concessions, unlawful seizure and confiscation of goods, and the expulsion from homes and land. In December, 1854, President Pierce informed Congress that numerous injuries by Mexicans to American citizens remained unadjusted and that new cases were constantly arising.[41] The many demands of the American

---

[37] Meriwether to Marcy, Nov. 29, 1854, Dept. of State, Misc. Let.

[38] From Charleston *Daily Courier*, Jan. 31, 1855.

[39] Almonte to Marcy, Feb. 15, 1855, Dept. of State, Notes to Dept., Mex. Leg., vol. 8.

[40] Davis to Marcy, Feb. 6, 1855, Dept. of State, Misc. Let.

[41] Richardson, *Messages and Papers of the Presidents*, V, 279.

claimants, Gadsden declared in September 1854, had converted the legation into an Attorney-general's office.[42]

It was only in regard to these claims that Marcy showed any concern, after the negotiation of the Gadsden treaty, for Mexican affairs. On May 29, 1854, he informed Gadsden that the United States would overlook some acts, but that the treatment of American citizens by Mexico was "repugnant to every principle of civilization and law."[43] Gadsden was directed to bring the matter to the attention of the Mexican government, which he did in a number of protests to Bonilla. On January 29, 1855, he furnished Bonilla with a list of American claims, and asked for a suggestion as to the mode of settlement.[44] These claims, Bonilla refused to entertain, and as a rebuttal, he presented Gadsden with a list of Mexican claims against the United States for filibustering expeditions and Indian raids into Mexico. Although Marcy constantly threatened that the indifference and neglect of the American claims by Mexico would lead to serious consequences, no action was taken by that government toward their settlement until 1868.

The Gadsden treaty did not stop the border troubles along the Rio Grande. The settlement of Wild Cat and his band of American Indians in Mexico added to the difficulties on the border, as his raids into Texas became more frequent after 1854.[45] Wild Cat held a commission in the Mexican army, and the Mexican officials encouraged in every way the incursions and robberies of the Indians in

[42] Gadsden to Marcy, Sept. 4, 1854, Dept. of State, Des., Mex., vol. 18, no. 40.

[43] Marcy to Gadsden, May 29, 1854, Dept. of State, Inst., Mex., vol. 17, no. 29.

[44] Gadsden to Bonilla, Jan. 29, 1855, Dept. of State, Des., Mex., vol. 19, with no. 57.

[45] See page 33.

Texas.[46]   These inroads resulted mainly in the destruction of plantations, the capture of slaves, and the theft of
animals.   Protests by Gadsden to the Mexican government,
against these incursions, were not considered by Bonilla.
He was surprised that Gadsden should impugn the officials
on the frontier with the robbery of a mule or horse when
thousands of such animals had been stolen from Mexican
territory by American Indians and sold to American
citizens.[47]

A second cause of border trouble arose out of the Mexican hostility to negro slavery in the United States and
the aid rendered by the Mexicans to fugitive slaves.   For
a small sum of money, Mexican citizens guided runaway
slaves into Mexico, where they were safe from pursuit,
as *cartas de seguridad* were freely given them by the
Mexican government.[48]   This aid to runaway slaves
assumed large proportions.   The legislature of Texas on
January 8, 1855, memorialized Congress for a mutual surrender with Mexico of criminals and slaves.[49]   The New
Orleans Commercial Convention of 1855 petitioned Congress for an extradition treaty with Mexico for the return
of fugitives from labor.[50]   In Texas the injured citizens
formed vigilance committees to protect their property.[51]

This Mexican aid to fugitive slaves was intolerable to
so strong a believer in slavery as Gadsden and he endeavoured to prevent the escape of slaves into Mexico.   A
circular was sent by him to the American consuls in Mexico, directing them not to certify to the citizenship of

[46] Smith to Cooper, Oct. 12, 1855, Dept. of State, Misc. Let.
[47] Bonilla to Gadsden, Nov. 7, 1854, Dept. of State, Des., Mex.,
vol. 18, with no. 50.
[48] Washington *Daily National Intelligencer*, Sept. 15, 1854.
[49] *S. Misc. Docs.* (563), 31 Cong., 1 sess., I, no. 101.
[50] Charleston *Daily Courier*, Jan. 19, 1855.
[51] Washington *Union*, Sept. 15, 1854.

negroes from the United States.[52] At the request of
Gadsden, Marcy furnished him with the authority to
negotiate an extradition treaty with Mexico.[53] Bonilla, at
the first suggestion, refused to consider the matter, but
through the proposition of Gadsden that the treaty would
include the return of Indian peons, who escaped into
Texas, he was moved, as Gadsden wrote, "to entertain
the subject which at first was so repugnant to the mis-
givings into which the agitation of African slavery had
misled and bewildered his mind."[54]   Some correspondence
ensued but no extradition treaty was made with Mexico
until 1861, and this did not include the extradition of
fugitive slaves.[55]

The federal military forces on the Mexican border
were unable to check the Indian inroads into Texas or to
prevent the escape of fugitive slaves.  As the Mexican
government had refused to interfere, the citizens of Texas
took matters into their own hands.  The population along
the border was of a type favorable to intervention in
Mexico, as it was composed mainly of two classes, merchants engaged in smuggling goods into Mexico, and
adventurers.[56]  The merchants, injured by the harsh tariff
laws of Mexico, were willing to promote invasions into
Mexico, and the wild and reckless adventurers on the
frontier were ready for a foray against either Indians or
Mexicans.  The product of these factors was a series of

[52] Copy of circular, with Gadsden to Marcy, July 3, 1854, Dept.
of State, Des., Mex., vol. 18, no. 33.

[53] Marcy to Gadsden, Dec. 3, 1853, Dept. of State, Inst., Mex.,
vol. 16, no. 17.

[54] Gadsden to Marcy, Nov. 5, 1854, Dept. of State, Des., Mex.,
vol. 18, no. 49.

[55] Malloy, *Treaties and Conventions*, I, 1125.

[56] A good discussion of the conditions on the border is found in
Rippy, J. F., "Border Troubles along the Rio Grande, 1848–60,"
in *Southwestern His. Quar.*, XXIII, 91–111.

counter-raids by the Texans into Mexico, two of which took place in the summer and fall of 1855.

The first of these movements was an abortive expedition led by Captain W. R. Henry. On July 18, 1855 he called upon the Texans to follow him as he went into Mexico to aid in the overthrow of Santa Anna and the establishment of a more republican form of government, favorable to the interests and prosperity of Texas, with the ultimate aim to make Mexico a protectorate of the United States.[57] His proclamation created much comment in the American and Mexican press, and caused a protest by Almonte to Marcy. The raid proved, however, to be a farce, as Henry was able to raise only fifty men, and he was informed by the Mexican officials that his men would be treated as marauders if they crossed the Rio Grande.[58]

A second expedition, which assumed larger proportions, was the invasion of Mexico in October, 1855, by Texans under the lead of Captain J. H. Callahan. This raid was a direct result of the inroads of Mexican Indians into Texas. In the summer of 1855, the Indians so increased their ravages, that Governor Pease was forced to call out the Texan volunteers, under the command of Captain Callahan.[59] Near the close of September, Callahan pursued a party of Indians across the Rio Grande, and on October 3, a skirmish ensued with a large party of Indians, assisted by Mexicans. Faced by a superior force, Callahan retreated, and in order to secure a safe retreat, burned the Mexican village of Piedras Negras.[60] The Mexicans pursued to the border, but were checked from further action by the commander of Fort Duncan,

[57] Copy of Henry's Proclamation, in N. Y. *Herald,* Aug. 17, 1855.
[58] Washington *Daily National Intelligencer,* Sept. 17, 1855.
[59] *Journal of the Senate of the State of Texas, Sixth Legislature,* 36.
[60] *Ibid.*

Captain Burbank, who, as he declared, in order to save life, pointed his cannon at the Mexican forces.[61]

This invasion occasioned immediate and continued protests from Almonte, who demanded the punishment of the Texan invaders and an indemnity for the destruction of Piedras Negras.[62]  Marcy denied that the act was a breach of neutrality, and informed Almonte that if Mexico would care for her Indians, there would be no intervention by the Texans.[63]  This inroad became a subject for diplomatic correspondence between the two governments during the remainder of the administration of President Pierce, but no action was taken until 1873, when the claimants for damages from the destruction of Piedras Negras were awarded an indemnity of $50,000.[64]

The vigilance of Brevet Major John E. Wool, Commander of the Department of the Pacific, put an end to further American filibustering expeditions into Mexico from California, but the raid of Count Raousset-Boulbon into Guaymas in 1854 occasioned a diplomatic skirmish.[65]  This French filibuster had led in 1852 an unsuccessful expedition into Sonora, but he retained the filibustering spirit and an opportunity for another adventure was furnished him by the Mexican government in 1854. Santa Anna believed that men were forced to take part in these raids because of poverty and lack of employment, and therefore, Del Valle, the Mexican consul at San Fran-

[61] Marcy to Almonte, Feb. 4, 1856, Dept. of State, Notes from Dept., Mex. Leg., vol. 7.

[62] Almonte to Marcy, Nov. 5, 1855, Dept. of State, Notes to Dept., Mex. Leg., vol. 8.

[63] Marcy to Almonte, Jan. 23, 1856: Feb. 4, 1856, Dept. of State, Notes from Dept., Mex. Leg., vol. 7.

[64] *S. Ex. Docs.* (1720), 44 Cong., 2 sess., III, no. 31, p. 10.

[65] The best study on the filibustering expeditions from California into Mexico, is Scroggs, W. O., *Filibusters and Financiers*.

cisco, was ordered on February 11, 1854, to send three thousand of the homeless men of San Francisco to Guaymas, where they were to be provided with land and were to become Mexican citizens.[66]    Three hundred and fifty Frenchmen were enlisted for Mexican service by Del Valle, and sent to Guaymas, where they were joined by Raousset-Boulbon, and under his leadership, the peaceful enterprise was changed into a filibustering expedition.    An attempt to capture Guaymas, however, resulted in the defeat of the Frenchmen and the capture and execution of Raousset-Boulbon.[67]

In the meantime, at San Francisco, Del Valle was arrested, on March 31, 1854, for the enlistment of men within the territory of the United States for the service of a foreign government.    His trial resulted in a verdict of guilty, but no sentence was given as the Federal District Attorney Inge dropped the case at that point.[68] Almonte protested against the trial of Del Valle.    He was surprised, he declared, that the same authorities of California, who manifested so much indifference when the expedition of Walker was set on foot, should be so zealous in the arrest of Del Valle, who had acted under the authority of his government.[69]    To a similar protest of Bonilla, Gadsden replied, that the aggrieved party in the Rousset-Boulbon affair was the United States, and he could not conceive that the American government was under any obligation to protect Mexico from French filibusters.[70]

[66] Almonte to Marcy, May 22, 1854, Dept. of State, Notes to Dept., Mex. Leg., vol. 8.

[67] Scroggs, *Filibusters and Financiers*, 61.

[68] Wool to Thomas, Mar. 31, 1854, *S. Ex. Docs.* (751), 33 Cong., 2 sess., VI, no. 16, p. 31.

[69] Almonte to Marcy, May 22, 1854, Dept. of State, Notes to Dept., Mex. Leg., vol. 7.

[70] Gadsden to Marcy, Aug. 1, 1854, Dept. of State, Des., Mex., vol. 18, no. 36.

The whole matter, soon settled by the execution of Boulbon and the release of Del Valle, is only a typical example of the petty issues that constantly arose between the two countries after the negotiation of the Gadsden treaty.

Another diplomatic controversy arose with Mexico over the commercial restrictions of Santa Anna. On his accession to power, Santa Anna proclaimed a new tariff, which almost prohibited the importation of foreign goods into Mexico.[71] His next move was to issue on January 30, 1854, a decree which imposed an additional duty of fifty per cent upon all goods imported into Mexico in foreign bottoms, not the manufacture and production of that nation.[72] In addition to these basic acts, there was a constant change of tariff rates. Pickett informed Marcy that it was impossible to send a copy of the existing tariff of the country because new revenue laws were decreed one day and revoked the next.[73]

These commercial restrictions tended to ruin American trade with Mexico and led to a series of protests from the American merchants in Mexico. Lobach and Schepelen declared that the navigation acts were designed to deliver the death blow to American commerce with Mexico.[74] Adams and Hickman asserted that it was impossible to introduce their goods into Mexico, as the duties would amount to eighty or ninety per cent of the original cost.[75] The American merchants at Tampico complained that

[71] Copy of tariff, in Conkling to Marcy, June 9, 1853, *ibid.*, vol. 17, no. 44.

[72] *Leyes, decretos y órdenes que formen el derecho internacional Mexicano*———656.

[73] Pickett to Marcy, Oct. 23, 1854, Dept. of State, Cons. Let., Vera Cruz, vol. 6.

[74] Lobach and Schepelen to Marcy, Mar. 22, 1854, Dept. of State, Misc. Let.

[75] Adams and Hickman to J. L. Collins, in Santa Fé *Weekly Gazette*, Nov. 19, 1855.

they received only the beggar's share of the Mexican trade, while England and France reaped the harvest.[76]

A demand arose in the southern states for a commercial treaty with Mexico. The New Orleans *Daily Picayune* declared that Gadsden had not yet accomplished the principal object of his mission, the negotiation of a commercial treaty with Mexico, so as to afford a profitable market for American commodities and valuable employment for American commerce.[77] The Charleston *Daily Courier* desired an arrangement with Mexico so that cotton, tobacco and other products might be introduced at a low rate of duty.[78] The New Orleans Commercial Convention in January 1855, recommended to the President and the Senate the establishment of a mutual commercial treaty with Mexico, whereby American products might be admitted into Mexico on equal terms with those of the most favored nation.[79]

Gadsden had early attempted to secure a treaty for better commercial relations between the two nations. In January 1855, he suggested to Bonilla, as a way to remove the border troubles, the framing of a reciprocity treaty, like that between the United States and Canada, but by May 1855, Gadsden informed Marcy that his attempts at commercial reconciliation led not to corrections, but only to further evasions on the part of Mexico. He advised, as the only remedy for the existing commercial situation, the deposition of Santa Anna by the United States.[80]

After the negotiation of the Gadsden treaty, there were constant references in the press in regard to a new treaty

[76] N. Y. *Herald,* Nov. 15, 1854.

[77] N. O. *Daily Picayune,* May 2, 1854.

[78] Charleston *Daily Courier,* Mar. 28, 1855.

[79] *Ibid.,* Jan. 19, 1855.

[80] Gadsden to Marcy, May 5, 1855, Dept. of State, Des., Mex., vol. 19, no. 62.

with Mexico.  The New York *Herald*  in an editorial, in
September 1854, on the revolutionary conditions in Mexico, declared that the policy initiated by the Gadsden
treaty for the gradual absorption of Mexico would soon be
continued by the administration.[81]   The same paper was
certain that Santa Anna would soon have to trade
or travel.[82]  The New York *Evening Post* considered
the acquisition of more Mexican territory as the only
practicable method to settle the question of claims with
Mexico.[83]

Gadsden, although it has been otherwise maintained,
was opposed to the purchase of further Mexican territory.[84]   ''I have declined,'' he declared, ''to be considered
a ministerial land jobber.'' [85]   The reports as to his negotiations on this subject he ascribed to the bankers who
were urging him to enter the market.  Gadsden desired
no land simply for the purpose of American expansion.
''I have said emphatically,'' he wrote Marcy, ''to all the
plundering cliques who approach me, that I will make no
treaty that does not right every wrong against the interests
and persons of the United States  .  .  .  I would purchase no land which would intimate that our Government
covets it.'' [86]   The absorption of Mexico, he thought would

[81] N. Y. *Herald,* Sept. 12, 1854.

[82] *Ibid.,* Feb. 19, 1855.

[83] From Charleston *Daily Courier,* Feb. 21, 1855.

[84] Callahan, J. M., ''The Mexican Policy of Southern Leaders
under Buchanan's Administration,'' in American Historical Association, *Annual Report, 1910,* 125–151.  The author here would show
that Gadsden favored the further acquisition of Mexican territory.
The quotations from the correspondence of Gadsden which are cited,
are taken out of their context, and give a very incorrect idea as to
the views of Gadsden.

[85] Gadsden to Marcy, July 11, 1855, Dept. of State, Des., Mex.,
vol. 19, unofficial.

[86] *Ibid.*

be the most irritating blister that could be placed on any body politic.[87]

The suggestion for a sale of Mexican territory to the United States came from Santa Anna, who in July and August, 1855, attempted to make a treaty with the United States, by which he might secure the necessary funds to continue his rule. For this purpose a conference was held July 8, 1855, between Santa Anna, Bonilla, and Gadsden. Santa Anna offered to mediate between Bonilla and Gadsden, and informed the latter that the note for his recall had been sent without his knowledge and that it would be immediately withdrawn.[88] Conferences were held almost daily for several weeks, and although Gadsden showed no great interest in the settlement of the issues, Bonilla appointed a commission to examine and adjust with Gadsden all the complaints and controversies between the two republics.

Gadsden characterized this move of Santa Anna as only an expedient to raise the wherewithal to sustain his power, and he objected to any action that would signify that the United States was in harmony with the government of Santa Anna.[89] "I cannot," he informed Marcy, "reconcile it to my judgment to negotiate with such a temporary oligarchy of plunderers."[90] To the offers of the Mexican commissioners for a sale of Mexican territory, Gadsden pursued a policy of procrastination.[91] All negotiations in this direction were defeated when on August 8, 1855, Santa Anna was forced to abdicate.

[87] *Ibid.* to *ibid.*, no date, but received Aug. 31, 1855, Dept. of State, Des., Mex., vol. 19, semi-official.

[88] *Ibid.* to *ibid.*, July 11, 1855, *ibid.*, vol. 19, unofficial.

[89] *Ibid.* to *ibid.*, Aug. 2, 1855, Marcy Papers, vol. 62.

[90] *Ibid.* to *ibid.*, no date, but received Aug. 31, 1855, Dept. of State, Des., Mex., vol. 19, semi-official.

[91] Lettsom to Clarendon, Aug. 2, 1855, F. O., Mex., vol. 279, no. 46.

Thus the diplomatic negotiations between the two countries, from the return of Gadsden to Mexico in June, 1854, to the abdication of Santa Anna in August, 1855, may be characterized as a series of petty quarrels. The Gadsden treaty had failed to secure the desired harmony of relations and all further attempts to settle the vexatious issues during this period had failed. The abdication of Santa Anna now gave Gadsden an opportunity to realize the hopes which he had entertained of amicable relations with Mexico under a Liberal government. Just as his influence had been in favor of the revolution, he now intended to see that a democratic government was established in Mexico, that would insure friendship between the two nations, and a respect on the part of Mexico for American citizens and institutions.

Upon the abdication of Santa Anna, the citizens of Mexico City declared for the Plan of Ayutla, but in the election for a provisional President the Conservatives were able to elect Martin Carrera, a former cabinet minister of Santa Anna, and an opponent of the revolution.[92] Although Álvarez and Comonfort, the revolutionary leaders, refused to recognize this election as fulfilling the Plan of Ayutla, Carrera was immediately recognized by the diplomatic corps, with the exception of Gadsden.[93] Because of his inability to maintain order, Carrera was forced to resign on September 12, 1855, and a general election, on October 4, 1855, according to the Plan of Ayutla, resulted in the choice of Álvarez as President *ad interim*.[94]

[92] N. Y. *Herald*, Sept. 4, 1855.

[93] Lettsom to Clarendon, Sept. 1, 1855, F. O., Mex., vol. 280, no. 63.

[94] Gadsden to Marcy, Oct. 19, 1855, Dept. of State, Des., Mex., vol. 19, no. 73.

Álvarez entered Mexico City on November 15, 1855, and immediately the new administration began an attack on the conservative classes.  A decree of November 30, abolished special military tribunals, removed the restrictions on the press, took away the privileges of the clergy, and annulled the exemption of church property from taxation.[95]  These reforms were bitterly opposed by the clergy and the army, and led immediately to a counter-revolution against the Liberals, which however was successfully put down.

Gadsden endeavoured to use his influence to make the new government democratic in nature, and to secure friendly relations between it and the United States.  He placed himself in close connection with the revolutionary leaders in the different parts of the republic, and sent agents to them, to aid in the establishment of a democratic régime.[96]  This activity of Gadsden called forth praise from the Liberal newspapers.  *El Monitor Republicano* lauded the diplomacy of Gadsden.  It gratefully remembered his suspension of relations with Santa Anna, and his refusal to recognize Carrera.[97]

This friendly attitude of Gadsden toward the Liberals was influenced also by his hostility to European activity in Mexico and South America.  As the European diplomats were, without exception, in league with the Conservatives, Gadsden would furnish American aid to the Liberals as a blow at foreign influence in Mexico.  "The Europeanizing of Mexico, of all South America," he informed Marcy, "in opposition to Anglo-American vandalism North of the Rio Grande has to be fought here." [98]

[95] N. Y. *Herald*, Dec. 19, 1855.

[96] Lettsom to Clarendon, Sept. 27, 1855, F. O., Mex., vol. 280, no. 72; Oct. 13, 1855, vol. 281, no. 91.

[97] *El Monitor Republicano*, Sept. 13, 1855.

[98] Gadsden to Marcy, Nov. 25, 1855, Dept. of State, Des., Mex., vol. 19, no. 77.

As a counter blow at Gadsden and in order to weaken the power of the Liberals, the Conservatives printed and broadcasted throughout Mexico a supposed treaty between Gadsden and Álvarez, by which Mexico was to become a protectorate of the United States.[99] In addition an American loan of $30,000,000 was to be made to Mexico, on the pledge of the property of the clergy and an American bank was to be established in Mexico, which was to control all internal improvements. This bogus treaty created considerable excitement in Mexico. Gadsden, because of the hostility to the United States, which the reported treaty occasioned in Mexico, was forced to make a public denial of its negotiation. In a letter to *El Monitor Republicano* on September 20, 1854, he denied in strong language that the United States desired a protectorate, and informed the Mexican people, as the New York *Herald* reported, "that the Government of the United States would see them damned first." [100]

The plan of Gadsden to democratize Mexico through the agency of Álvarez failed, because on December 8, 1855, Álvarez, on account of illness, resigned and appointed his fellow revolutionary chief, Ignacio Comonfort as substitute President.[101] Although Comonfort began his rule as a Liberal, he soon came under the control of the conservative classes. Friendship with Gadsden was abandoned and soon Gadsden compared Comonfort with Santa Anna, as "a usurped executive of one man will, resolving on falsifying the Plan of Ayutla, and like his predecessor dispos-

[99] Copy of the treaty is found in Lettsom to Clarendon, Sept. 18, 1855, F. O., Mex., vol. 20, no. 69.

[100] *El Monitor Republicano*, Sept. 20, 1855; N. Y. *Herald*, Oct. 18, 1855.

[101] Decree of Álvarez, with Gadsden to Marcy, Dec. 17, 1855, Dept. of State, Des., Mex., vol. 19, no. 79.

ing himself to the highest bidder.''[102]    The unfriendly
relations of Gadsden and Comonfort destroyed all further
attempts during the Pierce administration at diplomatic
reconcilation between the two nations.

With the revolution in Mexico, there arose again the
controversy over the payment of the $3,000,000 by the
United States to Mexico. Álvarez, immediately after the
overthrow of Santa Anna had protested to Gadsden
against the payment by the American government of the
$3,000,000 to the American bankers, and one of his first
official acts as President *ad interim* was to inform Secretary Marcy that the notes held by the American bankers
were null and void, and that the $3,000,000 should be
paid to Almonte.[103]    On December 10, 1855, a second protest was made. If the holders of the notes felt aggrieved,
they were at liberty, Almonte assured Marcy, to complain
to the government of Mexico, where their complaints
would receive consideration. The acceptance of these
drafts by the United States, he further asserted, would be
''a pretension too irreconcilable and so foreign to the
good understanding of the two republics.''[104]

The early attitude of Gadsden, following the revolution, was to urge Marcy to allow him to tender in advance
the $3,000,000 to the Liberals. Such an act he declared
would have a most favorable influence on the relations
between the two governments, as it would destroy the influence of Europe in Mexico, and would reconcile the
existing controversies between the United States and Mexico.[105]    But with the increasing conservatism of the Mexi-

[102] Gadsden to Marcy, Oct. 4, 1856, *ibid.*, vol. 19, no. 97.
[103] Almonte to Marcy, Nov. 3, 1855, Dept. of State, Notes to Dept.,
Mex. Leg., vol. 8.
[104] *Ibid.* to *ibid.*, Dec. 10, 1855, *ibid.*
[105] Gadsden to Marcy, no date, shortly after Santa Anna abdicated, Marcy Papers, vol. 66.

can government, Gadsden changed his policy, and on December 5, 1855, he advised Marcy to withhold indefinitely the payment of the $3,000,000, because it was the only lever that remained in the hands of the legation to bring the Mexican government to a just sense of her treaty responsibilities to the United States.[106]

At Washington, the agents of Hargous Brothers and Howland and Aspinwall, demanded that Secretary Marcy authorize the payment of their drafts.[107] They argued that the bonds were valid, that the boundary line had already been surveyed, even if the monuments were not as yet placed, and that the revolution in Mexico did not invalidate their drafts. Marcy accepted their view, and Almonte was informed that the drafts were considered valid by the American government. He was therefore asked to withdraw the protest of his government.[108]

The Mexican government was loath to lose any opportunity to acquire money, and therefore in order to secure the withdrawal of the protest, the American speculators were forced to grease the palms of the Mexican officials. Howland and Aspinwall complained to Marcy that the Mexican protest was only a scheme to extract a large sum of money from the American draft holders.[109] A compromise was made, by which, according to Gadsden, the Mexican government was given $500,000 by the American note holders for the withdrawal of the protest.[110] The

---

[106] *Ibid.* to *ibid.*, Dec. 5, 1855, Dept. of State, Des., Mex., vol. 19, no. 78.

[107] Shepherd to Marcy, Oct. 27, 1855, Marcy Papers, vol. 64; Nov. 4, 1855, vol. 65; Dec. 1, 1855, vol. 65; no date, vol. 74.

[108] Marcy to Almonte, Nov. 29, 1855, Dept. of State, Notes from Dept., Mex. Leg., vol. 7.

[109] Howland and Aspinwall to Marcy, Jan. 23, 1856, Dept. of State, Misc. Let.

[110] Gadsden to Marcy, Dec. 5, 1855, Dept. of State, Des., Mex., vol. 19, no. 78.

protest was withdrawn by Almonte in February, 1856, and subsequently, the $3,000,000 was paid to the holders of the Mexican drafts.[111]

The payment of these drafts by the administration occasioned another quarrel between Gadsden and Marcy. Gadsden was unable to see how President Pierce could back up the holders of the drafts.[112]  He denounced the whole affair as another Ward case, and declared that difficulties with Mexico were increased by the protection extended by the American government to this great fraud.[113]  When Gadsden returned to the United States in May, 1856, on a leave of absence, he informed the British minister at Mexico City that he "would show up and expose Mr. Marcy for having sold himself in the matter of the recent payments of the Mesilla Treaty money." [114]

Immediate steps were taken by the new Mexican government, for the establishment of better commercial relations with the United States.  In September, 1855, the Ceballos tariff was restored and the obnoxious commercial decrees of Santa Anna were annulled.[115]  The removal of the prohibition on tobacco and concessions to freer commercial interests on the Mexican border, Gadsden informed Marcy in January, 1856, had greatly tended to the settlement of the disturbing issues in that quarter.[116]  On January 31,

[111] *S. Ex. Docs.* (821), 34 Cong., 1 & 2 sess., XII, no. 57, p. 76.

[112] Gadsden to Marcy, Apr. 5, 1856, Dept. of State, Des., Mex., vol. 19, no. 87.

[113] *Ibid.* to *ibid.*, Apr. 18, 1856, *ibid.*, vol. 19, no. 88.

[114] Lettsom to Clarendon, June 1, 1856, F. O., Mex., vol. 291, no. 98.

[115] Pickett to Marcy, Sept. 8, 1855, Dept. of State, Cons. Let., Vera Cruz, vol. 6.

[116] Gadsden to Marcy, Jan. 25, 1856, Dept. of State, Des., Mex., vol. 19, no. 83.

1856, a new tariff, liberal in principle, was decreed by President Comonfort.[117]

Gadsden again attempted to secure a commercial treaty with Mexico but his endeavours, as hitherto, proved unsuccessful. All that he was able to accomplish was the negotiation of a postal convention, which provided for a free postal intercourse between the two countries. This convention, however, which Gadsden was certain would operate a most important change in the Mexican prohibitions and restrictions against free commerce, was not ratified by either country.[118]

The commercial reforms attempted by the Mexican government proved of little permanent value. The commercial relations at the close of the administration of President Pierce, despite the many efforts of Gadsden to secure a change, remained as they had since the Mexican War. On this subject, Pickett wrote in December 1856, that, "the continued revolutionary state of the Republic, the absurd laws enacted, and the general paralization of commerce renders the above a very unfruitful and unsatisfactory theme. Until the establishment of a stable government, the commercial history of this country will present nothing but a series of disasters and a state of decadence coexistent with its unfortunate political status." [119]

The subject of Mexican claims under article XI of the treaty of Guadalupe Hidalgo was reopened in 1856 by the Mexican government. On May 27, 1856, Pezeula, the successor of Almonte, addressed a lengthy note to Marcy on this topic and presented the view that the Gadsden treaty

[117] Copy of Comonfort tariff, with Pickett to Marcy, Feb. 10, 1856, Dept. of State, Cons. Let., Vera Cruz, vol. 6.

[118] Gadsden to Campbell, Aug. 4, 1856, Dept. of State, Des., Mex., vol. 19, with no. 94.

[119] Pickett to Marcy, Dec. 31, 1856, Dept. of State, Cons. Let., Vera Cruz, vol. 6.

relieved the United States only from the obligation to execute article XI in the future.[120]   The United States, he affirmed was still responsible for the depredations of the American Indians prior to the negotiation of the treaty, and therefore he demanded for his government an adequate indemnity for the Mexicans who had suffered from Indian inroads.   Marcy rejected Roble's interpretation of article XI and declared that: "if any liability were attached to the United States under the 11th article of the treaty of 1848—a fact always denied by this government, they were in no doubtful language released by the 2nd article of the treaty of 1853." [121]   This subject was not finally settled until 1873, when the American-Mexican Claims Commission accepted the view maintained by Marcy in 1856, and the Mexican claims were disallowed.[122]

After the abdication of Santa Anna, the hostility of the American speculators in Mexico toward Gadsden became more intense, because he consistently refused to aid them in their schemes.   To the request of P. A. Hargous for the aid of the legation in the Garay affair, Gadsden replied that he felt no obligation to make an issue with the Mexican government over the subject.[123]   In like manner, he refused to aid the Sloo Company, and asserted that he would not give a straw for the eighth article of his treaty. An agent of the Sloo Company described Gadsden as "so deadly hostile to the Tehuantepec grant, that he talked like a partisan on the other side." [124]   American soldiers

[120] Bezeula to Marcy, May 27, 1856, Dept. of State, Notes to Dept., Mex. Leg., vol. 8.

[121] Marcy to Pezeula, July 9, 1856, Dept. of State, Notes from Dept., Mex. Leg., vol. 7.

[122] Moore, *History and Digest of International Arbitrations*, III, 2444–2447.

[123] Gadsden to Marcy, Apr. 18, 1856, Dept. of State, Des., Mex., vol. 19, no. 88.

of fortune of every type found it impossible to work their schemes through the agency of Gadsden.

This increased hostility of the speculators to Gadsden was shown in their many attempts to destroy his influence in Mexico and to secure his removal as minister. The New York *Herald* declared that, "it is those who profit by Mexican speculation that fight to remove Gadsden." [125] Of the influence of American speculators in foreign countries, Pickett declared that, "here in Mexico the whole matter is painfully illustrated. We have a minister, able, patriotic and courageous, but 'tis generally understood he is Perry-ized; (so to speak) by a power behind the throne. His best endeavours are rendered nugatory." [126] Gadsden charged that the policy of the administration toward Mexico was dominated by the speculators, and that private individuals, instead of the legal representative had the ear of Marcy.[127] The intriguing of these speculators against Gadsden was one of the causes for his recall as minister in June, 1856.

Another factor in the recall of Gadsden was the mutual animosity between Gadsden and Comonfort. Accordingly, on May 9, 1856, the removal of Gadsden was demanded by the Mexican government. He was charged with meddling in domestic affairs, with uttering improper censures against, and creating serious obstacles to the progress of the Mexican government. He was declared to be an impediment in the way of pacific relations between the two countries and the recall of Gadsden, Pezeula asserted, would be another assurance of American friend-

[124] Private Memorandum on Mexican affairs, Sept. 22, 1855, no name signed, Marcy Papers, vol. 63.

[125] N. Y. *Herald*, June 27, 1856.

[126] Pickett to Marcy, Mar. 22, 1856, Dept. of State, Cons. Let., Vera Cruz, vol. 8.

[127] Copy of letter, in N. Y. *Herald*, Apr. 10, 1856.

ship to Mexico.[128]    The administration yielded to this request and on June 30, Gadsden was informed of his recall by Marcy, but was asked to remain in Mexico until the arrival of his successor.[129]

It is impossible to state the relative proportion which the influence of the speculators and the demands of the Mexican government played in the removal of Gadsden. During the months of May and June, when the demand for the recall of Gadsden was being considered by President Pierce, there were constant references in the press in regard to the lobby of American speculators and Mexican officials working in Washington to have Gadsden removed from office.[130]    Upon the announcement of the recall of Gadsden, the New York *Herald* declared that Ward would be sent as Secretary of the Mexican legation, ''inasmuch as he, knowing more than anyone else of certain transactions in Mexico, will not tell tales out of school.''[131]    The strained relations between Gadsden and Marcy may have influenced President Pierce to comply with the request of the Mexican government.    Gadsden placed the blame for his recall upon Marcy.  He wrote to Buchanan that, ''our foreign relations  .  .  .  particularly with Mexico have been so mystified and besotted by our would-be premier, that I fear that much of complications will be left for your administration.  Advices on my part, indeed remonstrances, have only involved me in issues with our foreign office, which after unsuccessful efforts to Souleize me out of position has resulted in my recall.''[132]    Again he asserted

128 Pezeula to Marcy, May 9, 1856, Dept. of State, Notes to Dept., Mex. Leg., vol. 8.

129 Marcy to Gadsden, June 30, 1856, Dept. of State, Inst., Mex., vol. 17, no. 65.

130 N. Y. *Herald,* June 29, 1856; Baltimore *Sun,* June 27, 1856.

131 N. Y. *Herald,* June 30, 1856.

132 Gadsden to Buchanan, Aug. 2, 1856, Buchanan Papers.

that the demand for his recall by the Mexican government was due to his vigilance in discovering European intrigues in Mexico, which was unacceptable to Comonfort.[133] In his valedictory dispatch to Marcy, he exonerated himself from all responsibility for the possible loss of Mexico, Cuba, and the Gulf of Mexico to the United States, through the ascendancy of European influence in those regions.[134]

Gadsden remained as minister in Mexico until October, 1856, when he was replaced by James Forsythe of Mobile, Alabama. In his last note to Fuente, Minister of Foreign Relations, Gadsden declared that he had hoped to break off relations without any feelings of dissatisfaction or disappointment, but that the hostile note of October 20, from the Mexican Department of Foreign Relations, could not permit such to be the case. He informed Fuente that the insulting note was received, and reciprocated in the same spirit in which it was sent, whether it came officially from the Mexican government or privately from the minister of Foreign Relations.[135]

It was only toward the close of Pierce's term of office that a firm attitude was exhibited toward Mexico by the administration. Forsythe was urged in his instructions to produce in the minds of the government and people of Mexico a feeling that the United States had no sinister designs on that nation; and in order to establish better relations, both political and commercial with Mexico, he was instructed to negotiate a postal convention, adjust the American claims against Mexico, and secure a revision of

---

[133] Gadsden to Marcy, Oct. 4, 1856, Dept. of State, Des., Mex., vol. 19, no. 97.

[134] *Ibid.*

[135] Gadsden to Fuente, Oct. 23, 1856, *ibid.*, vol. 19, with no. 100.

the Mexican tariff.[136]  In his last annual message to
Congress, December 2, 1856, President Pierce declared
that it was against Mexico that our complaints for damages
to American citizens were most numerous.  Only the dis-
turbed political conditions of Mexico, he informed Congress, had caused forbearance on the part of the United
States toward that nation.[137]  Marcy, also, who had neglected to answer the long dispatches of Gadsden, and had
refused to consider his advice, was in 1857, aroused from
his lethargy as to Mexico.  In his last note to Pezeula
Marcy complained of the many injuries to American
citizens in Mexico, and of the failure of Mexico to make
redress in a single case.  His policy, he declared had been
to withstand the strong appeais of his countrymen for
counter measures against Mexico, with the hope that
Mexico would right these wrongs.  The present condition
of affairs could not continue, and if Mexico were unable
and unwilling to redress past, present, and future injuries
to American citizens, Marcy declared it would be ''the
right as well as the duty of the United States to adopt such
measures as may seem best calculated to secure to them the
quiet and undisturbed enjoyment of their rights whenso-
ever they are threatened or invaded by the authorities of
that Republic or its respective states.'' [138]

[136] Marcy to Forsythe, Aug. 16, 1856, Dept. of State, Inst., Mex.,
vol. 17, no. 2.
[137] Richardson, *Messages and Papers of the Presidents,* V, 414.
[138] Marcy to Pezeula, Feb. 5, 1857, Dept. of State, Notes from
Dept., Mex. Leg., vol. 7.

# CHAPTER VII

## CONCLUSION

In conclusion, while the purpose of this study has been to furnish a detailed account of the antecedents, negotiation, ratification and aftermath of the Gadsden treaty, it will be remembered that the treaty was not an isolated incident of American history in the period in which it was negotiated. For instance, the isthmian question, a topic of speculation since the European colonization of the western hemisphere, became connected in the nineteenth century with the commercial expansion of the United States in the Orient, and involved Anglo-American isthmian rivalry, and American imperialism in the tropics. The agitation for an American transcontinental railroad and its influence on the negotiation of the Gadsden treaty is only one phase of the westward expansion of the American people in the first half of the nineteenth century. The need to relieve the United States from the responsibility for damages, resulting from the inroads of the American Indians into Mexico, is also closely connected with the larger Indian question that faced the American government in the period, 1840–1860, which involved other matters, such as a transcontinental railroad, slavery and sectionalism. The role played in the framing of the treaty by speculators is only one indication of the trend of American business men of that period toward the exploitation of enterprises in foreign countries and their demand for governmental support and protection.

Even from the merely diplomatic standpoint, as has already been indicated, the Gadsden treaty, must not be viewed as a single, disconnected achievement, but rather as a product of the vigorous foreign policy of the first two years of Pierce's administration. How long and to what an extent this policy would have been continued toward Mexico, can only be surmised, for after 1854, with the revival of the slavery controversy, foreign affairs in general, became a secondary matter. The issues with Mexico, unsettled by the Gadsden treaty and the other controversies which arose after 1854, coupled with the great need of money by Santa Anna, certainly offered an opportunity for another treaty with Mexico, which would have involved the cession of further Mexican territory. The administration, in view of the sectional struggle, saw the futility of such an attempt and after the ratification of the Gadsden treaty, little attention was given to Mexican affairs.

The Gadsden treaty, although it may be classed partly as a result of the expansionist tendencies of the Pierce administration, cannot be interpreted solely as a scheme to aid the South through the acquisition of new slave territory. Von Holst, however, has described the purchase of Mexican territory as another scheme of the slavocracy. On this subject he writes: ''There is no reason for the assumption that, with Pierce, the desire to give the slavocracy a new and broad domain was decisive. All that he personally wanted was to make an important acquisition of territory. But, as a matter of course, he was sure that the slavocracy would claim that territory, and he as well as the slavocracy, considered it as good as certain that it would actually fall to their share. . . . The 'great principle' of the Kansas-Nebraska bill was a blank draft handed to the south by the north with its signature, and the first word that the South tried to write in it was not

Kansas but northern Mexico.''[1]   The bias of von Holst
is clearly shown, when it is recalled that the first instructions to Gadsden of July 15, 1853 and the instructions of
October 22, 1853, carried by Ward to Gadsden, antedated
by several months, the introduction of the Kansas-
Nebraska bill into Congress.   The treaty was already
negotiated when the bill which repealed the Missouri
Compromise act became a law.   Again, the attempted expansion of the United States and the vigorous foreign
policy of President Pierce were not directed alone toward
the south, but extended in all directions.   American foreign affairs were not in the control of southern men, but
were directed by a President from New Hampshire, and a
Secretary of State from New York, while on the other
hand, the American minister to Mexico, although a
southern slaveholder, considered that a large acquisition
of Mexican territory by the United States, except for a
natural boundary, would be a national mistake.   Although
the expansion of slavery was not the cause for the negotiation of the treaty, the opposition to slavery in the United
States, revived by the introduction of the Kansas-Nebraska
question, almost defeated its ratification.

While von Holst's explanation is shown by the facts
already stated to have been incorrect, there is no doubt
that there was prevalent an element of expansion in the
instructions to Gadsden for the purchase of Mexican territory.   The vigorous foreign policy, in contrast with the
vacillating attitude of President Fillmore, which characterized the administration of President Pierce, was in
keeping with the general tendency toward militant expansion that dominated the mind of the American people during the period, 1840-1860.   A favorable opportunity was

---

[1] Von Holst, H., *The Constitutional and Political History of the
United States*, V, 7-9.

offered in the existing situation in Mexico for the United States to secure the territory which President Polk had failed to acquire in the treaty of Guadalupe Hidalgo, and although Pierce did not pursue such a bold expansionist policy at the expense of Mexico, as that which his successor, Buchanan, later attempted, it can safely be assumed that his larger plans included more than the acquisition of a mountain range for a boundary between the two nations. The mistake of von Holst is his identification of national expansion with the supposed aggression of the slavery interests.

The Gadsden treaty failed to secure for the United States those advantages desired by the administration, which had been the bases for the negotiation of the treaty. This failure however was not due to the inadequacy of the provisions of the treaty, but was rather on account of the overshadowing of foreign issues by domestic questions in the United States after 1854. Although sufficient Mexican territory was purchased for a transcontinental railroad route on American soil, sectionalism, increasing after the passage of the Kansas-Nebraska act, blocked every effort for the construction of a railroad on any of the proposed routes. The treaty also did not secure for the United States, an interoceanic connection by the way of the Isthmus of Tehuantepec. The protection which was guaranteed by article VIII to the Sloo Company was never given. Although all attempts at the construction of the isthmian connection were defeated, partly by the rivalry of the two companies, and partly by the hostility of the Mexican government, the Mexican policy of President Buchanan was closely connected with the isthmian question, and was determined to a considerable extent by the agents of the Sloo and Hargous companies. The Gadsden treaty did not suddenly halt the predatory raids of the American Indians into Mexico. Border troubles increased during the administration of President Buchanan, and the injuries inflicted by Mexicans upon American citizens in Texas, and the territory of New Mexico, were assigned by Buchanan in December, 1858, as a reason why the United States should assume a temporary protectorate over the border states of Mexico. The boundary survey under the Gadsden treaty also proved unsatisfactory and a relocation of the boundary line was necessitated in 1882.[2]

A study of the Gadsden treaty furnishes a picture of the political and economic conditions of Mexico, in the decade following the Mexican War. It shows a repetition by the Mexican government after the war of its former policy of procrastination and stubbornness in the settlement of any difficulty with the United States. It was due to the continuance of civil wars in Mexico, the great need of money by the existing government, and the fear of a war

[2] The 29,142,400 acres of land acquired under the Gadsden treaty, described by the senators in 1854 as worthless territory, can be considered the greatest advantage which the United States secured from the treaty. The purchase of this area for the sum of $10,000,-000, has proved to be a great bargain. This territory is included within the states of New Mexico and Arizona. The second, third, and fourth cities in Arizona, as to wealth and population, Tucson, Douglas, and Bisbee, are in the region of the Gadsden Purchase. Cochise county, Arizona, alone has an assessed value of $160,000,000. The greatest future development of agriculture in Arizona will be in the area included in the territory purchased from Mexico. However the political stupidity of the United States Senate in 1854, in its refusal to secure a boundary line which included a port on the Gulf of California, has retarded the development of this region and of the whole southwest. With the increased agricultural production of Arizona a demand has arisen, as Gadsden predicted in 1854, for an outlet to the Gulf of California. To this end, a memorial was introduced in the last session of the legislature of Arizona for the purchase from Mexico of a strip of territory, contiguous to Arizona, along the Gulf of California.

with the United States, that the treaty was successfully negotiated. The Gadsden treaty, was, therefore, from the Mexican standpoint, only made possible by these conditions, which were able to overcome the hostility of the Mexican government for the United States. The money received by Mexico under the treaty was immediately squandered by Santa Anna. Except for the averting of a possible war with the United States, the treaty gave no benefits to the Mexican people.

In brief, it may be said that a detailed study of the Gadsden treaty warrants the following general conclusions. The treaty was in a large degree, a product of the spirit of the age in the United States, while the conflicting interpretations of the treaty of Guadalupe Hidalgo furnished the immediate causes for its negotiation. Therefore, it can be viewed partly as a business deal between the two nations and partly as a result of the American expansionist tendencies in the period, 1840–1860. It was closely connected with the other diplomatic achievements, resulting from the militant foreign policy of the Pierce administration. The negotiation of the treaty had no direct connection with the expansion of the institution of slavery. American speculators and European diplomats attempted to use sinister influences in its negotiation and ratification. Only the disorganized political and financial conditions of Mexico made possible its negotiation. Because of sectional feeling and the efficient lobbying of speculators, favorable action by the Senate on the treaty was secured only after it had been materially amended; and the treaty as changed by the Senate, was accepted by President Pierce and Santa Anna, only on the grounds of expediency. Accordingly the Gadsden treaty immediately became the basis for new diplomatic issues between the two nations, and it proved a failure as an instrument for a better relationship between the sister republics, and a definitive settlement of the Mexican question.

# BIBLIOGRAPHY

## I. GUIDES AND BIBLIOGRAPHIES

Bolton, H. E., *Guide to Materials for the History of the United States in the Principal Archives of Mexico*, Carnegie Institution of Washington, Publication No. 163, Washington, 1913.

Channing, E., A. B. Hart, and F. J. Turner, *Guide to the Study and Reading of American History*, revised and augmented edition, Boston, 1912.

Hasse, A. R., *Index to United States Documents Relating to Foreign Affairs, 1828–1861*, Carnegie Institution of Washington, Publication No. 185, 3 vols., Washington, 1914–1921.

————*Reports of Explorations Printed in the Documents of the United States Government*, Washington, 1899.

Library of Congress-Division of Manuscripts, *Check List of Collections of Personal Papers in Historical Societies, University and Public Libraries and other Learned Institutions in the United States*, Washington, 1918.

Library of Congress-Division of Manuscripts, *Handbook of Manuscripts in the Library of Congress*, Washington, 1918.

Library of Congress-Periodical Division, *A Check List of American Newspapers in the Library of Congress*, Washington, 1901.

Library of Congress-Periodical Division, *A Check List of Foreign Newspapers in the Library of Congress*, Washington, 1904.

Morrison, H. A., *List of Books and of Articles in Periodicals Relating to Interoceanic Canals and Railway Routes*, Washington, 1900.

New York Public Library-Bulletin, Vol. 5, *Manuscript Collections in the New York Public Library.* Vol. 20, *Bibliography of American Interoceanic Canals.*

Parker, D. W., *Calendar of Papers in Washington Archives Relating to Territories of the United States (to 1873),* Carnegie Institution of Washington, Publication No. 148, Washington, 1911.

Paullin, C. O., and F. L. Paxson, *Guide to the Materials in London Archives for the History of the United States since 1783,* Carnegie Institution of Washington, Publication No. 90–B, Washington, 1914.

United States Document Office, *Checklist of United States Public Documents, 1789–1909, Congressional: to close of 60th Congress, Departmental: to end of Calendar Year 1909,* 3rd edition, Washington, 1911.

Van Tyne, C. H., and W. G. Leland, *Guide to the Archives of the Government of the United States in Washington,* second edition, Carnegie Institution of Washington, Publication No. 92, Washington, 1907.

## II. MANUSCRIPT SOURCES

### (I). Official

Department of State, Division of Publications.
   Consular Letters,
         Acapulco, vols. 1–3.
         Chihuahua, vol. 1.
         Matamoras, vol. 6.
         Mazatlán, vol. 2.
         Mexico City, vol. 10.
         Tehuantepec, vol. 1.
         Vera Cruz, vol. 6.
   Despatches—Mexico, vols. 14–20.
   Domestic Letters, vols. 41–42.
   Instructions—Mexico, vols. 16–17.
   Miscellaneous Letters, March 1853–August 1854.
   Notes from Department—Mexican Legation, vols. 6–7.
   Notes to Department—Mexican Legation, vols. 7–8.
   Opinions—United States and Mexican Claims Commission, 1868, vol. III.
   Special Agents—C. L. Ward, Package.

Special Missions, No. 3, Memorandum of Instructions
    to C. L. Ward, October 22, 1853.
Public Record Office, London.
    Foreign Office—America, Despatches, vols. 593, 597,
        616, 617, 618, 639.
    Foreign Office—Mexico, Despatches, vols. 260, 261,
        267, 268, 275, 276, 277, 279.
    Foreign Office—Mexico, Instructions, vol. 265.
    An attempt was made by the author to examine the
    Mexican official documents that relate to the Gadsden
    treaty.   Both Professor H. T. Collings of the Uni-
    versity of Pennsylvania and Miss A. M. Blake of
    Mexico City personally endeavoured to secure the
    materials, but on account of the present condition of
    the Mexican archives, they were unsuccessful in their
    efforts.

### (II). Unofficial

Bartlett, John R. Papers: John Carter Brown Library.
Bell, John.  Papers: Library of Congress.
Buchanan, James.  Papers: Library of Historical Society
    of Pennsylvania.
Clayton, John M.  Papers: Library of Congress.
Crittenden, John Jordan.  Papers: Library of Congress.
Davis, Jefferson.  Papers: Library of Congress.
Donelson, Andrew J.  Papers: Library of Congress.
Fillmore, Millard.  Papers: Library of Congress.
Gadsden, James.  Papers: New York Public Library.
Green, Duff.  Papers: Library of Congress.
Hammond, James H.  Papers: Library of Congress.
Jackson, Andrew.  Papers: Library of Congress.
Johnston, J. S.  Papers: Library of Historical Society of
    Pennsylvania.
Marcy, William L.  Papers: Library of Congress.
Mason, James M.  Papers: Virginia State Library.
Monroe, James.  Papers: New York Public Library.
Pierce, Franklin.  Papers: Library of Congress.
Poinsett, Joel R.  Papers: Library of Historical Society
    of Pennsylvania.
Polk, James K.  Papers: Library of Congress.
Trist, Nicholas P.  Papers: Library of Congress.
Webster, Daniel.  Papers: Library of Congress.

## III. PRINTED SOURCES

### (I). PUBLIC DOCUMENTS

*American State Papers, Indian Affairs,* 4 vols., Washington, 1832.
*American State Papers, Military Affairs,* 7 vols., Washington, 1832–1861.

### CONGRESSIONAL

THE NUMBER BETWEEN THE PARENTHESES IS THE SERIAL
NUMBER OF THE VOLUME OF THE
CONGRESSIONAL DOCUMENTS.

*Congressional Globe,* 30 Cong., 1 sess., 1847–48, XVIII; 30
Cong., 1 sess., 1847–48, App., XIX; 30 Cong., 2 sess.,
1848–49, XX; 31 Cong., 1 sess., 1849–50, XXI; 31
Cong., 1 sess., 1849–50, App., XXII; 31 Cong., 2 sess.,
1850–51, Globe and App., XXIII; 32 Cong., 1 sess.,
1851–52, XXIV; 32 Cong., 1 sess., 1851–52, App.,
XXV; 32 Cong., 2 sess., 1852–53, XXVI; 32 Cong.,
2 sess., 1852–53, App., XXVII; 33 Cong., 1 sess.,
1853–54, XXVIII; 33 Cong., 1 sess., 1853–54, App.,
XXIX.
*Journal of the Executive Proceedings of the Senate of the
United States of America,* I–IX, Washington, 1828–87.
*Senate Executive Documents.*
    30 Cong., 1 sess., III (505), No. 7.  Notes of a military reconnaissance from Fort Leavenworth, in
    Missouri, to San Diego, in California.  Brevet
    Major W. H. Emory.
    30 Cong., 1 sess., IV (506), No. 23.  Report of Lieut.
    J. W. Abert of his examination of New Mexico
    in the years, 1846–1847.
    30 Cong., 1 sess., VII (509), No. 52.  Correspondence
    relating to, and the proceedings of the United
    States Senate in regard to the treaty of Guadalupe Hidalgo.
    30 Cong., 1 sess., VII (509), No. 60.  Correspondence
    in relation to the treaty of Guadalupe Hidalgo
    and recommendations for its enforcement.

31 Cong., 1 sess., I (549), No. 1. Annual message to Congress, Pres. Z. Taylor, Dec. 4, 1849; Report of the Secretary of War, G. W. Crawford, Nov. 30, 1849.

31 Cong., 1 sess., II (550), No. 1. Report of the Secretary of the Interior, T. Ewing, Dec. 3, 1849.

31 Cong., 1 sess., X (558), No. 34. Report on operations of the United States-Mexican boundary commission.

31 Cong., 1 sess., XIV (562), No. 64. Report of the Secretary of War, S. J. Anderson, with reconnaissance of routes from San Antonio to El Paso; also the report of Captain R. B. Marcy's route from Fort Smith to Santa Fé and the report of Lieut. J. H. Simpson of an expedition into the Navajo country and the report of Lieut. W. H. C. Whiting's reconnaissance of the western frontier of Texas.

31 Cong., 2 sess., I (587), No. 1. Annual message to Congress, Pres. M. Fillmore, Dec. 2, 1850; Report of the Secretary of the Interior, A. H. H. Stuart, Dec. 2, 1850; Report of the Secretary of War, C. M. Conrad, Nov. 30, 1850.

32 Cong., 1 sess., I (611), No. 1. Annual message to Congress, Pres. M. Fillmore, Dec. 2, 1851; Report of the Secretary of War, C. M. Conrad, Nov. 29, 1851.

32 Cong., 1 sess., III (613), No. 1. Report of the Commissioner of Indian Affairs, L. Lea, Nov. 27, 1851.

32 Cong., 1 sess., IX (620), No. 60. Report on charges against John R. Bartlett.

32 Cong., 1 sess., IX (620), No. 80. Papers on claim of Samuel A. Belden against the government of Mexico.

32 Cong., 1 sess., IX (620), No. 89. Report on the McClellan-Bartlett controversy.

32 Cong., 1 sess., X (621), No. 97. Correspondence between United States and Mexico relative to a right of way across the Isthmus of Tehuantepec.

32 Cong., 1 sess., XIV (626), No. 119. Correspond-

ence relative to the United States-Mexican boundary line controversy.

32 Cong., 1 sess., XV (627), No. 121. Report of Lieut. Colonel Graham on the United States-Mexican boundary survey.

32 Cong., 1 sess., XV (627), No. 120. Correspondence of De la Vega and Secretary Webster on United States-Mexican boundary survey.

32 Cong., 1 sess., III (637), No. 15. Message in regard to last installment of indemnity due Mexico, Pres. M. Fillmore.

32 Cong., 2 sess., I (658), No. 1. Annual message to Congress, Pres. M. Fillmore, Dec. 6, 1852; Report of the Secretary of the Interior, A. H. H. Stuart, Dec. 4, 1852.

32 Cong., 2 sess., II (659), No. 1. Report of the Secretary of War, C. M. Conrad, Dec. 4, 1852.

32 Cong., 2 sess., III (660), No. 14. Correspondence relative to encroachment of American Indians upon Mexico.

32 Cong., 2 sess., III (660), No. 16. Report on United States-Mexican boundary survey, Secretary of the Interior, A. H. H. Stuart, Jan. 10, 1853.

32 Cong., 2 sess., III (660), No. 17. Correspondence in regard to imprisonment of American citizens at Acapulco, Mexico.

32 Cong., 2 sess., III (660), No. 23. Report on removal of Florida Indians to the country west of the Mississippi, Secretary of the Interior, A. H. H. Stuart, Jan. 14, 1853.

32 Cong., 2 sess., VII (665), No. 41. Report of J. R. Bartlett on the boundary line between the United States and Mexico.

33 Cong., Special session, (688), No. 6. Report of the Secretary of the Interior, R. McClelland, communicating papers in relation to the United States-Mexican boundary commission.

33 Cong., 1 sess., I (690), No. 1. Annual message to Congress, Pres. F. Pierce, Dec. 5, 1853; Report of the Secretary of the Interior, R. McClelland, Dec. 5, 1853.

33 Cong., 1 sess., II (691), No. 1. Report of the Secretary of War, J. Davis, Dec. 1, 1853.

33 Cong., 1 sess., III (692), No. 1. Report of Postmaster General Campbell, Dec. 1, 1853.

33 Cong., 1 sess., IV (694), No. 2. Report of the Secretary of the Treasury, James Guthrie, Dec. 6, 1853.

33 Cong., 1 sess., V (695), No. 29. Report on Pacific Railroad Routes, Secretary of War, J. Davis.

33 Cong., 1 sess., VIII (698), No. 52. Report on Pacific Railroad Routes, Secretary of War, J. Davis.

33 Cong., 2 sess., I (746), No. 1. Annual message to Congress, Pres. F. Pierce, Dec. 4, 1854; Report of the Secretary of the Interior, R. McClelland, Dec. 4, 1854.

33 Cong., 2 sess., II (747), No. 1. Report of the Secretary of War, J. Davis, Dec. 4, 1854.

33 Cong., 2 sess., VI (751), No. 13. Report by R. H. Schoolcraft on the state of Indian statistics.

33 Cong., 2 sess., VI (751), No. 16. Correspondence between the War Department and Maj. General Wool, in regard to his operations on the Pacific Coast.

33 Cong., 2 sess., VI (751), No. 21. Report on diplomatic service, Secretary of State, W. L. Marcy, Jan. 10, 1855.

33 Cong., 2 sess., VI (751), No. 25. Correspondence between Maj. General Wool and the different departments of the government in relation to American filibustering expeditions into Mexico.

33 Cong., 2 sess., VII (752), No. 55. Report of Capt. A. B. Gray, relative to the United States-Mexican boundary survey.

33 Cong., 2 sess., XIII, pts. 1–11 (758–768), No. 78. Pacific Railroad Reports.

    I (758). Report of Secretary of War, J. Davis, on the routes.

    II (759). Report of Lieut. Colonel W. H. Emory.

    III (764). Report of Lieut. John G. Parke.

XI (768). Memorial of Lieut. G. K. Warren. Account of exploring expeditions since 1800 from the Mississippi River to the Pacific Ocean. Topographical maps to illustrate reports on the Pacific Railroad Routes.

34 Cong., 1 & 2 sess., II (811), No. 1. Report of Secretary of War, J. Davis, Dec. 3, 1855.

34 Cong., 1 sess., XII (821), No. 57. Report of Secretary of State, W. L. Marcy, on the United States-Mexican boundary line and the payment of the $3,000,000 under the Gadsden treaty to Mexico.

34 Cong., 1 sess., I–III (832–834), No. 108. Report on the United States-Mexican boundary survey, Major W. H. Emory.

34 Cong., 3 sess., VIII (881), No. 51. Report of Captain Thomas J. Cram on the oceanic routes to California.

35 Cong., 1 sess., XIII (930), No. 72. Correspondence between the United States and Mexico relative to the Isthmus of Tehuantepec.

44 Cong., 2 sess., III (1720), No. 31. Claims on the part of citizens of the United States and Mexico under the convention of July 4, 1868.

55 Cong., 2 sess., XXIII–XXV (3612–3614), No. 247. Report on the United States-Mexican boundary survey, 1891–1896.

*Senate Miscellaneous Documents.*

30 Cong., 2 sess., I (533), No. 50. Petition of P. A. Hargous in regard to the Tehuantepec grant.

31 Cong., 1 sess., I (563), No. 101. Resolution of the Texas legislature in favor of an extradition treaty with Mexico.

32 Cong., 2 sess. (670), No. 5. Memorial of Little Rock Railroad Convention in favor of a southern Pacific railroad.

32 Cong., 2 sess. (670), No. 33. Memorial of F. W. Rice, regarding Mexican outrages upon American citizens at Acapulco.

32 Cong., 2 sess. (670), No. 36. Memorial of the legislature of New Mexico, in favor of a transcontinental railroad.

32 Cong., 2 sess. (670), No. 52. Petition of the President of Vicksburg, Shreveport and Texas Railroad Company for land grants in aid of railroads, Feb. 1, 1853.

*Senate Reports.*

32 Cong., 1 sess., II (631), No. 344. Report on the memorial of Robert Mills for a railroad connection with the Pacific Ocean.

32 Cong., 1 sess., II (631), No. 345. Report on initial point in boundary line between the United States and Mexico.

32 Cong., 1 sess., II (631), No. 355. Report of Committee on Foreign Relations on right of way across the Isthmus of Tehuantepec.

32 Cong., 2 sess. (671), No. 401. Report of select committee on the United States-Mexican boundary line.

33 Cong., 1 sess., II (707), No. 353. Report on compensation of William Rich, Secretary of the United States legation in Mexico.

33 Cong., 1 sess., II, pt. 2 (708), No. 182. Report of select committee on the proceedings of the Board of Commissioners on the claims against Mexico.

34 Cong., 3 sess., I (891), No. 440. Report on memorial of M. O. Roberts in regard to mail contracts of A. G. Sloo.

*House Executive Documents.*

31 Cong., 1 sess., VIII (577), No. 62. Correspondence between the United States and Mexico relative to the American Indians on the Mexican border.

32 Cong., 1 sess., II, pt. 2 (635), No. 2. Report of the Secretary of the Interior, A. H. H. Stuart, Nov. 29, 1851.

32 Cong., 1 sess., V (640), No. 32. Report on the remaining installments of the Mexican indemnity.

32 Cong., 1 sess., V (640), No. 42. Correspondence in reference to payment of the Mexican indemnity.

32 Cong., 1 sess., XII (648), No. 112. Report on disorders on Rio Grande frontier, Secretary of State, Daniel Webster.

33 Cong., 2 sess., IV (782), No. 15. Information in regard to the Creek and Seminole Indians on the Texas border.

33 Cong., 1 sess., XIII (726), No. 109. Message of President Pierce, June 20, 1854, accompanied by Gadsden treaty.

*House Miscellaneous Documents.*

33 Cong., 1 sess. (741), No. 38. Letters addressed to the Committee on Indian affairs, transmitting and explaining estimates for Indian appropriations.

33 Cong., 1 sess. (741), No. 45. Memorial of Legislative Council of New Mexico on the Indians in New Mexico.

*House Reports.*

31 Cong., 1 sess., II (584), No. 280. Report of Committee on Indian Affairs on Indian incursions into Mexico, Apr. 24, 1850.

31 Cong., 1 sess., III (585), No. 439. Memorial of the Memphis Convention of 1849, accompanied by report of Committee on Naval Affairs on a railroad to the Pacific.

33 Cong., 2 sess. (808), No. 142. Case of B. E. Green vs. T. H. Bayly, in regard to payment of Mexican indemnity.

33 Cong., 2 sess. (808), No. 151. Report on the Indian depredations in Texas.

Malloy, W. M., *Treaties, Conventions, International Acts, Protocols and Agreements Between the United States and Other Powers,* 2 vols., Washington, 1910.

Moore, J. B., *A Digest of International Law as embodied in Diplomatic Discussions, Treaties and other International Agreements, International Awards, . . . of the United States,* 8 vols., Washington, 1906.

——*History and Digest of the International Arbitrations to which the United States has been a Party,* 6 vols., Washington, 1898.

Richardson, J. D., *Compilation of the Messages and Papers of the Presidents, 1789–1897*, 10 vols., Washington, 1896–1899.

*The Statutes at Large of the United States of America*, I–IX (to 1855), Boston, 1845–1856.

United States Department of State Publications. *United States and Mexican Claims Commission under Convention of July 4, 1868*, vol. 1. Memorials and Briefs.

United States Department of State Publications. *United States and Mexican Claims Commission under Convention of July 4, 1868*, vol. II, *Rafael Aguirre and 365 other Claims against the United States*, Evidence, Briefs, and Arguments.

## STATE

*Journal of the House of Representatives of the State of Texas, 1853–1854*, Austin, 1853.

*Journal of the Senate of the State of Texas, Sixth Legislature*, Austin, 1855.

## MEXICO

Archivo Mexicano. *Actos de las sesiones de las Cámaras, Despacho Diario de los Ministerios, succesos notables, Documentos Oficiales importantes y rectificación de hechos oficiales*, Tom. I, num. III; Tom. II, num. I, IV.

México. *Colección de las leyes fundamentales que han regido en la República Mexicana, y de los planes que han tenido mismo carácter, desde el año de 1821 hasta él de 1856*, México, 1856.

México. *Leyes, decretos y órdenes que forman el Derecho Internacional Mexicano o que se relacionan con el mismo*, Edición Oficial, México, 1879.

México. *Tratados y convenciones concluidos y ratificados por la República Mexicana, desde su independencia hasta el año actual, acompañados de varios documentos que les son referentes*. Segunda Parte. *Tratados y convenciones celebrados y no ratificados por la República Mexicana*, Edición Oficial, México, 1878.

México: Congreso. *Documentos relativos a la apertura de una vía de comunicación inter-océanica por el istmo Tehuantepec, mandamos imprimir por acuerdo de la Camara de Diputados*, México, 1852.

México: Congreso, Senado. *Dictamen de la comisión especial de Tehuantepec del Senado, encargado de examinar las varias resoluciones dictadas con motivo del privilegio exclusivo concedido a D. José Garay.* México, 1851.

México: Ministerio de Relaciones Interiores y Exteriores. *Decreto del supremo gobierno para la apertura del istmo de Tehuantepec, contrato celebrado con la compañía mixta y comunicaciones diplomáticas relativas al asunto,* México, 1853.

México: Ministerio de Relaciones Interiores y Exteriores. *Statement of the right and just reasons on the part of of the Government of the United States of Mexico for not recognizing either the subsistence of the privilege granted to D. José Garay for the opening of a line of communication between the Atlantic and Pacific seas, through the Isthmus of Tehuantepec or the legality of the cession which he made of said privilege to the United States,* Mexico, 1852.

República Mexicana. *Informes y Manifestos de los poderes ejecutivo y legislativo de 1821 a 1904,* Vol. I, *Mensajes y sus respuestas desde 28 de Septiembre de 1821 hasta 31 de Mayo de 1863,* México, 1905.

Palacio, F. G., *Claims of Mexican Citizens against the United States for Indian Depredations, being the Opinion of the Mexican Commissioner in the Joint Claims Commission under the convention of July 4, 1868, between Mexico and the United States,* Washington, 1871.

Santa Anna, Antonio López de, *Manifesto del Presidente de la República a la Nación,* México, 1855.

Santa Anna, Antonio López de, *El Presidente de la República a sus Concuidadanos, December 17, 1853,* México, 1853.

(II) UNOFFICIAL COLLECTIONS

Abel, A. H., *The Official Correspondence of James S. Calhoun while Indian Agent at Santa Fé and Superintendent of Indian Affairs in New Mexico,* Washington, 1915.

Coleman, C., *The Life of John J. Crittenden, with selections from his correspondence and speeches,* 2 vols., Philadelphia, 1871.

Crallé, R. K., *The Works of John C. Calhoun,* 6 vols., New York, 1853–1855.

Jameson, J. F., *Correspondence of John C. Calhoun,* in American Historical Association, *Annual Report, 1899,* II, Washington, 1900.

Moore, J. B., *The Works of James Buchanan,* 12 vols., Philadelphia, 1908–1911.

Quaife, M. M., *The Diary of James K. Polk, during his Presidency, 1845–1849,* 4 vols., Chicago, 1910.

Pereyra Garciá y Carlos, *Documentos—O muy raros para la Historia de Méjico,* Tomo II, Santa Anna, Antonio López de, *Mi Historia militar y política 1810–1874, Memorias Inéditas,* México, 1905.

Ray, P. O., "Some Papers of Franklin Pierce, 1852–62," in *American Historical Review,* X, 110–127; 350–370.

Rowland, D., *Jefferson Davis, Constitutionalist, His Letters, Papers, and Speeches,* 10 vols., New York, 1923.

Severance, F. H., *Millard Fillmore Papers,* in *Buffalo Historical Society Publications,* X–XI, Buffalo, 1907.

Van Tyne, C. H., *The Letters of Daniel Webster,* New York, 1902.

## (III) NEWSPAPERS

### AMERICAN

California.
    *Alta California* (San Francisco).
District of Columbia.
    *Washington Daily National Intelligencer.*
    *Washington Union.*
Florida.
    *Pensacola Gazette and West Florida Advertiser.*
    *St. Augustine East Florida Herald.*
    *The Floridian and Advocate* (Tallahassee).
    *The Floridian* (Tallahassee).
Georgia.
    *Augusta Daily Chronicle and Sentinel.*
    *Savannah Daily Republican.*
Indiana.
    *Daily Indiana State Sentinel* (Indianapolis).
Louisiana.
    *New Orleans Daily Picayune.*

Michigan.
*Detroit Free Press.*
New Mexico.
*Santa Fé Weekly Gazette.*
New York.
*Albany Argus.*
*New York Herald.*
*New York Journal of Commerce.*
*New York Times.*
*New York Tribune.*
Ohio.
*Cincinnati Daily Enquirer.*
Pennsylvania.
*Philadelphia North American and United States Gazette.*
*Philadelphia Public Ledger.*
South Carolina.
*Charleston Daily Courier.*
Tennessee.
*Memphis Daily Eagle and Enquirer.*
*Nashville Union and American.*
*Republican Banner and Nashville Whig.*
Texas.
*Texas State Gazette* (Austin).
Virginia.
*Richmond Enquirer.*

### FOREIGN.

England.
*London Times.*
Mexico.
*Boletín Oficial del Supremo Gobierno.*
*Centinela-Periódico Oficial de Chihuahua.*
*Diaria Oficial del Gobierno de la República Mexicana.*
*El Comercio de Tampico.*
*El Monitor Republicano.*
*El Orden.*
*El Siglo y Nueve.*
*El Universal.*

## (IV) MONOGRAPHS AND SPECIAL WORKS

Abel, A. H., "History of Indian Consolidation West of the Mississippi," in American Historical Association, *Annual Report, 1906*, I, Washington, 1908.

Albright, G. L., *Official Explorations for Pacific Railroads, 1853–55*, Berkeley, 1921.

Arrangoiz, F. de P., *El Istmo de Tehuantepec*, México, 1852.

Butler, P., *Judah P. Benjamin*, Philadelphia, 1916.

Bartlett, J. R., *Personal Narrative of Explorations and Incidents in Texas, New Mexico and Chihuahua, connected with the United States and Mexican Boundary Commission, during the years, 1850, '51, '52, and '53*, 2 vols., New York, 1854.

Curtis, G. T., *Life of Daniel Webster*, 2 vols., New York, 1870.

Davis, C. H., *Report on Interoceanic Canals and Railroads between the Atlantic and Pacific Oceans*, Washington, 1867.

Davis, J. P., *The Union Pacific Railway; a study in railway politics, history and economics*, Chicago, 1894.

Davis, V. J., *Jefferson Davis, Ex-President of the Confederate States: a Memoir*, 2 vols., New York, 1890.

Dexter, F. B., *Biographical Sketches of the Graduates of Yale College with Annals of the College History*, 6 vols., New Haven, 1912.

Dodd, W. E., *Jefferson Davis*, Philadelphia, 1907.

————*Statesmen of the Old South*, New York, 1911.

Donaldson, T. C., *The Public Domain: its History with Statistics with Reference to the National Domain, Colonization, Acquirement of Territory . . . revised July 16, 1881*, Washington, 1881.

Farrish, T. B., *History of Arizona*, 8 vols., Phoenix, 1915–1918.

Garay, J. de., *An Account of the Isthmus of Tehuantepec in the Republic of Mexico; with proposals for establishing a communication between the Atlantic and Pacific Oceans, based upon the surveys and reports of a scientific commission appointed by the projecter, Don José de Garay*, London, 1846.

Gittinger, R., *The Formation of the State of Oklahoma, (1803–1906)*, Berkeley, 1917.

Goodwin, C., *The Trans-Mississippi West, 1803–1853: A history of its acquisition and settlement,* New York, 1922.

Hamer, P. M., *The Secession Movement in South Carolina, 1847–1852,* Allentown, 1918.

Haney, L. H., *The Congressional History of Railways in the United States,* Madison, 1908–1910.

Hawthorne, N., *Life of Franklin Pierce,* Boston, 1852.

Jervey, T. D., *The Railroad, the Conqueror,* Columbia, 1913.

——————*Robert Y. Hayne and His Times,* New York, 1909.

Larrainzar, M., *La Cuestión de Tehuantepec. Contiene dos notas del enviado extraordinario y ministerio plenipotenciario de la república Mexicana en Washington, y algunos artículos que sobre esta materia se han publicado,* New York, 1852.

Malin, J. C., *Indian Policy and Westward Expansion,* Kansas University Series of Humanistic Studies, vol. 2, No. 3, Lawrence, 1921.

Marshall, T. M., *A History of the Western Boundary of the Louisiana Purchase, 1819–1841,* Berkeley, 1914.

McCormac, E. I., *James K. Polk, A Political Biography,* Berkeley, 1922.

McElroy, R. McN., *The Winning of the Far West; a history of the regaining of Texas, of the Mexican War, and the Oregon question; and the successive additions to the territory of the United States, within the continent of America: 1829–1869,* New York, 1914.

McKitrick, R., *The Public Land System of Texas, 1823–1910,* Madison, 1918.

Meigs, W. M., *The Life of John Caldwell Calhoun,* 2 vols., New York, 1917.

Meyer, B. H., and C. E. MacGill and a staff of collaborators, *History of Transportation in the United States before 1860,* Carnegie Institution of Washington, Publication No. 215c, Washington, 1917.

Olasagarre, M., *Cuenta de la percepción, distribución e inversion de los diez milliones de pesos que produjo el tratado de la Mesilla, celebrado por el gobierno supremo de la república con el de los Estados Unidos de América en 13 de dicembre de 183,* México, 1855.

Payno, M., R. Olarte y J. Pesado., *Cuestión de Tehuantepec*, México, 1852.

Phillips, U. B., *A History of Transportation in the Eastern Cotton Belt to 1860*, New York, 1908.

Portilla, A. de la, *Historia de la revolución de México contra la dictadura del General Santa Anna, 1853–1855*, México, 1856.

Potts, C. S., *Railroad Transportation in Texas*, Bulletin of the University of Texas, No. 119, Humanistic Series, No. 7, Austin, 1909.

Ramírez, J. F., *Memorias, negociaciones y documentos para servir a la historia de las diferencias, que han suscitado entre México y los Estados Unidos, los tenedores del antiguo privilegio, concedido para la comunicación de los mares Atlántico y Pacifico por el istmo de Tehuantepec*, México, 1852.

Reeves, J. S., *American Diplomacy under Tyler and Polk*, Baltimore, 1907.

Rives, G. L., *The United States and Mexico, 1821–1848*, 2 vols., New York, 1913.

Scroggs, W. O., *Filibusters and Financiers, The Story of William Walker and his Associates*, New York, 1916.

Smalley, E. V., *History of the Northern Pacific Railroad*, New York, 1893.

Smith, J. H., *The Annexation of Texas*, New York, 1911.
————*The War with Mexico*, 2 vols., New York, 1919.

Stanwood, E., *A History of the Presidency from 1788 to 1897*, Boston, 1898.

Thompson, W., *Recollections of Mexico*, New York, 1846.

Twitchell, R. E., *The Leading Facts of New Mexico History*, 2 vols., Cedar Rapids, 1911–1912.

White, H. K., *History of the Union Pacific Railway*, Chicago, 1895.

Williams, M. W., *Anglo-American Isthmian Diplomacy, 1815–1915*, Washington, 1916.

Wooten, D. G., *A Comprehensive History of Texas, 1685–1897*, 2 vols., Dallas, 1898.

## (V) MAGAZINE ARTICLES

Binkley, W. C., "The Question of Texan Jurisdiction in New Mexico under the United States, 1848–50," in *Southwestern Historical Quarterly*, XXIV, 1–38.

Blount, B., "The Apache in the Southwest," in *Southwestern Historical Quarterly*, XXIII, 20–39.

Boucher, C. S., "The Annexation of Texas and the Bluffton Movement in South Carolina," in *Mississippi Valley Historical Review*, VI, 3–33.

————"In Re that Aggressive Slavocracy," in *Mississippi Valley Historical Review*, VIII, 13–80.

————"The Secession and Coöperation Movements in South Carolina, 1848 to 1852," in *Washington University Studies, Humanistic Series*, V, 97–111.

Callahan, J. M., "The Mexican Policy of Southern Leaders under Buchanan's Administration," in American Historical Association, *Annual Report, 1910*, 125–151.

Cotterill, R. S., "The Beginnings of Railroads in the Southwest," in *Mississippi Valley Historical Review*, VIII, 318–326.

————"Early Agitation for a Pacific Railroad, 1845–50" in *Mississippi Valley Historical Review*, V, 396–415.

————"Memphis Railroad Convention, 1849," in *Tennessee Historical Magazine*, IV, 83–95.

————"Southern Railroads and Western Trade, 1840–50," in *Mississippi Valley Historical Review*, III, 427–441.

Cox, I. J., "The Southwestern Boundary of Texas," in *Quarterly of the Texas State Historical Association*, VI, 82–102.

Crane, R. C., "Some Aspects of the History of West and Northwest Texas since 1845," in *Southwestern Historical Quarterly*, XXVI, 30–43.

Dallas, G. M., "Isthmus of Tehuantepec," in *Journal of Franklin Institute*, Third Series, XII, 15–21.

Ellison, W. H., "The Federal Indian Policy in California," in *Mississippi Valley Historical Review*, IX, 37–67.

Gadsden, J., "The Commercial Spirit of the South," in *De Bow's Commercial Review*, II, 117–133.

Gittinger, R., "The Separation of Nebraska and Kansas from the Indian Territory," in *Mississippi Valley Historical Review*, III, 442–461.

Goodwin, C., "The Question of the Eastern Boundary of California in the Convention of 1849," in *Southwestern Historical Quarterly*, XVI, 227–258.

Learned, H. B., "Cabinet Meetings under President Polk," in American Historical Association, *Annual Report, 1914*, I, 229–242.

Marshall, T. M., "The Southwestern Boundary of Texas, 1821–1840," in *Quarterly of the Texas State Historical Association*, XIV, 278–293.

Mayes, E., "Origin of the Pacific Railroads, and especially of the Southern Pacific," in *Publications of the Mississippi Historical Society*, VI, 307–337.

Moore, J. B., "A Great Secretary of State," in *Political Science Quarterly*, XXX, 377–396.

Muckelroy, A., "The Indian Policy of the Republic of Texas," in *Southwestern Historical Quarterly*, XXVI, 1–29; 128–148.

Paxson, F. L., "The Pacific Railroads and the Disappearance of the Frontier in America," in American Historical Association, *Annual Report, 1907*, I, 105–122.

Ramsdell, C. W., "Internal Improvement Projects in Texas in the Fifties," in *Proceedings of the Mississippi Valley Historical Association*, IX, 99–109.

————"The Public Lands and the Indians in Texas, 1846–59," in *Mississippi Valley Historical Review*, VIII, 9.

Reeves, J. S., "The Treaty of Guadalupe Hidalgo" in *American Historical Review*, X, 309–325.

Rippy, J. F., "Anglo-American Filibusters and the Gadsden Treaty," in *Hispanic American Historical Review*, V, 155–181.

————"Border Troubles along the Rio Grande, 1848–60," in *Southwestern Historical Quarterly*, XXIII, 91–111.

————"Diplomacy of the United States and Mexico Regarding the Isthmus of Tehuantepec, 1848–60," in *Mississippi Valley Historical Review*, VI, 503–532.

————"The Indians of the Southwest in the Diplomacy of the United States and Mexico, 1848–53," in *Hispanic American Historical Review*, II, 363–396.

————"A Ray of Light on the Gadsden Treaty," in *Southwestern Historical Quarterly*, XXIV, 235–242.

————"The Boundary of New Mexico and the Gadsden Treaty," in *Hispanic American Historical Review*, IV, 715–742.

Sears, L. M., "Slidell and Buchanan," in *American Historical Review*, XXVII, 709–730.

Sioussat, St. G. L., "Memphis as a Gateway to the West. A Study in the Beginnings of Railroad Transportation in the Old Southwest," in *Tennessee Historical Magazine*, III, 1–28; 77–115.

————"Southern Projects for a Railroad to the Pacific Coast, 1845–1857." An unpublished paper read before the American Historical Association, at New Haven, Connecticut, December 29, 1922.

Taggart, F. J., "The Approaches to California," in *Southwestern Historical Quarterly*, XVI, 63–75.

Winkler, E. W., "The Cherokee Indians in Texas," in *Quarterly of the Texas State Historical Association*, VII, 95–165.

## (VI) GENERAL WORKS

The American Nation: A History. Edited by A. B. Hart. Garrison, G. P., *Westward Extension*, New York, 1906. Smith, T. C., *Parties and Slavery*, New York, 1906.

Bancroft, H. H., *History of Arizona and New Mexico, 1530–1888*, San Francisco, 1889.

————*History of Mexico, 1516–1887*, 6 vols., San Francisco, 1883–1888.

————*History of the North Mexican States and Texas*, 2 vols., San Francisco, 1889.

McMaster, J. B., *A History of the People of the United States from the Revolution to the Civil War*, 8 vols., New York, 1888–1913.

Rivera, M., *Historia Antigua y Moderna de Jalapa y de las Revoluciones del Estado de Vera Cruz*, 5 vols., México, 1869–1871.

Rhodes, J. F., *History of the United States from the Compromise of 1850*, 8 vols., New York, 1893–1919.

Schouler, J., *History of the United States of America under the Constitution*, 6 vols., New York, 1880–1899.

Von Holst, H., *The Constitutional and Political History of the United States*, trans. by J. J. Lalor and A. B. Mason, 8 vols., Chicago, 1877–1892.

Zamacois, N. de, *Historia de Méjico desde sus tiempos más remotos hasta nuestros días*, 23 vols., México, 1876–1902.

# INDEX

207